Rigs Pigs & Dirty Digs

Barry J Steel

ISBN: 978-1-326-12239-3

BARRY J STEEL

AUTHOR OF

THAILAND AFTER DIVORCE

RIGS, PIGS & DIRTY DIGS

With thanks to Sharon,
in one night you
turned me from a
boy into a man

"I'm flying through a cloudy haze,
Edging closer to the waves,
And each rig looks the same to me,
The faces and surrounding sea,
It reminds me that I long to be,
Homeward bound…"

BJ/PS

CONTENTS

PART THREE- THE TENS

INTRODUCTION

Dear reader, I want to start by thanking you for purchasing this book. (Handbook is probably a better description, my apologies for the thickness) If you have purchased this book after reading my debut then I want to tell you that you've made me genuinely happy. I almost feel like I've robbed you!

This book is a completely different beast to my first. Although I was happy and proud of my debut, I realised that there was a little bit too much serious stuff in there and in life I'm not a serious person at all. With this book I have three goals in mind, I want to try and make you laugh, shock you and if it's at all possible even educate you a tiny bit.

I went through a few titles before deciding on the one you see on the cover, *'Porn, Prostitutes and Prohibited Substances'* and *'A Perverts Guide to Life'* were two of my favourites, but I had a feeling that those titles would put a lot of married men off buying it.

This book doesn't have a linear narrative like my first one does, it's a collection of mildly amusing and sordid stories from my life and also a collection of rants about the many, many things that I hate! Also this time round there's no holding back, all the restraint that I showed in my first book is gone. I have gone out of my way to humiliate myself in this book, with no shame whatsoever, all for your reading pleasure. So please enjoy. If you finish this book with a smile on your face then I'll have achieved my goal. If you don't then you must just be a miserable, dour faced twat!

I placed a warning in my first book that it was not a book for women. Again I'll put a warning in this book but this one is slightly longer. I really don't like upsetting people so if you are any of the following please don't read any more of this book: a woman, a gypsy, religious, offended by swear words/drug use/ racist jokes, ginger, pathetic, shy, nervous and most importantly…if you can't handle the cold, hard TRUTH!

PART ONE

THE NINETIES

1
PORN - A CHILDHOOD STORY

Dear reader, as I write these words I feel like weeping! Oh, how I could literally weep when I think of these kids today. They walk around with a device in their pockets that enables them to 24 hours a day free access to pornography… but they will never have the same experiences that we all got to have when we were their age. That feeling of complete and utter excitement and naughtiness after finding a muddy, soiled porn magazine stashed in a bush or some woods. Fighting amongst your friends to see who could look at it first and then fighting again when the braver boys wanted to sneak it home. The kids of today will never know what it felt like to secretly watch a mucky VHS tape in their parent's house. The completely shit quality of the picture, the painfully slow fast forwarding which sent blurry lines across the screen.

In fact the stuff that these kids of today watch is so extreme that a plain old anal scene won't even register in their minds! But not for us, when we first saw those anal scenes our hearts missed a beat. Those surgical close up shots where all you could really see was some bloke's hairy arsehole and balls slapping about. Then cut to the extreme close up of a woman's face, screaming in ecstasy as her huge perm bounced around. And what about those older kids who told us they'd seen a video of a woman with two men? One in the minge and one in the bullethole at the same time! LIARS! We would call them, until we finally saw it for ourselves, the disbelief in our little faces as our jaws hung slack. These kids of today really don't know what they've missed out on.

There's a question that I've always wanted to know the answer to. Just who were those dirty bastards who stashed porn mags in bushes? For some reason we all imagine them to be dirty old men but if you sit and think about it, why would a grown man go to a shop, buy a porno and then head straight to the nearest bush? Surely they would just take it to the comfort of their own home. We will never know the answer.

I want to admit straight away that I'm a complete porn addict. In fact I really couldn't imagine life without porn. It's always there for you when you need it, a bad day at work, an argument with the wife or even when your head feels fragile after a night out. A good wank will always sort you out.

Apart from the aforementioned finding stashed mags in bushes, my own personal porn story began at the age of thirteen. On my thirteenth birthday my older brother told me he had a present for me. He lifted the mattress on his bed to reveal four porn mag's neatly laid in a row. He told me that I could pick whichever one I wanted. (Still to this day it's the nicest thing he's ever done for me, the rest of the time he was an absolute cunt!) The magazine I picked was a Parade, I can't remember the issue number but it had a woman with short blonde hair on the front, I think there was a swimming pool behind her. (It's worth pointing out that I was already wanking by this stage but thus far had had to make do with fantasies of shagging the girls in my class. Usually bent over a table in an empty classroom.) This was my first completely clean magazine, there was no mud, no pages stuck together and best of all I didn't have to share it with anyone…it was all mine! I lovingly kept it in the space below my bottom drawer.

It's strange how such a tiny little moment like this could trigger the start of a life of debauchery and perversion. We've all been there, we've all had this moment. I wonder, did we all turn out to be such perverts?

Just look at what we masturbate over today. Even double anal seems tame these days. It appears that all the big name stars have to do at least one golden shower scene and now a blowjob isn't a blowjob unless the girl is turning blue in the face and fighting back vomit. Of course if you want to see the vomit then that's just a click of a button away as well. (Have you noticed that when people post porn vids they always try to come up with a funny title? Only one has ever made me laugh, the image was a close up of a double anal and the caption read 'Three people in love' Class!) I have a mate who's just as addicted to porn as I am and he said to me recently,

"Imagine if we'd known what was to come when we were younger? Free porn! More than you could ever watch in a lifetime!"

If somebody had told us back then I don't think we would've believed them. This mate is one of my closest friends and our friendship was built on porn. There was a time when we only knew each other a little bit but it wasn't until we swapped some porn vid's that our friendship truly blossomed. What a wonderful thing porn is, it brings people together. Maybe all those Sunni's and Shiite's should have a mass DVD swap, then they would realise that we're all the same. All just dirty bastards!

Whilst having ideas for this book and scribbling down notes I've realised how similar we all are as a male species. We've all had the same experiences and thoughts. Who can say that when they were at school they didn't accidently call a female teacher mam? Who can say that when they were sat in a classroom without desks they weren't guaranteed to get a hard on? For me it was always music. We would sit in a semi-circle, boys on one side and girls on the other. This just made it even worse! When the erection came you knew that the teacher was going to ask you to stand up at any minute. Blindly fiddling through your trouser pocket to make it point upwards and then untucking your shirt, even though the first thing the teacher was going to say was '*Tuck your shirt in!*' Oh the shame!

These days I don't possess a single porn DVD, it's the evolution of porn. I got rid of all my mags when I'd built up a healthy VHS collection. I said goodbye to the VHS's when DVDs came out and now we all have it on our mobiles, it was time to get shot of the DVDs. In fact watching it on a telly seems strange these days, I'm just used to it being on a small screen a few inches away from my face. Of course the main benefit of mobile porn is you don't need to hide it in a cupboard from the other half. There's no chance of her walking in on you, as you look for the DVD remote in blind panic with your trousers around your ankles. We always used to get caught.

I wonder what the next stage of porn evolution will be? A 4D headset with some sort of sucking device strapped our manhood? We can only wait and dream. One day this generation of kids will grow up and they will moan to the next generation about having to put up with porn on their mobiles! They really don't know that they're born!

Dear reader, you are quickly going to realise that the chapters in this book are short. I've decided that at no point do I want to take the risk of boring you. I'm going to say all that needs to be said and then move on. Think of this book as a literary version of the Fast Show, if you find yourself disliking a particular chapter then don't worry you will soon be onto the next one. You'll find each chapter is completely different from the one before. If you've found that all this reminiscing about porn has given you a trouser twitch then please do not hesitate to knock one off now. You'll feel a lot better for it, I promise. (Unless you're in a public place of course, I can't be held responsible for your actions!).

2
PROSTITUTES PART ONE THE EARLY YEARS

Dear reader, I couldn't even to begin to guess how many prostitutes I've been with in my life, I just know it's a lot! I've forgotten probably 90% of them, the ones I do remember I usually remember for bad reasons. These are the ones you are going to hear about in this book. I'll forewarn you that my experiences with 'ladies of the night' in the 1990's didn't really amount to much, but every story must have a beginning.

I lost my virginity at the age of seventeen, if you're wondering '*why so old?*' then you need to know that I was one of those kids who always looked young for his age. I didn't get pubes till the end of second year and at the age of seventeen I looked more like a fourteen year old. (A message to all you men who showed off your hairy chests in first year. Ha-ha! You were all bald by the time you were twenty, you shiny headed cunts!)

My first foray into the murky world of prostitution happened at the age of sixteen and it happened completely by accident. A friend and I were walking the dark Middlesbrough streets after leaving a house party. We ventured onto a street notorious for street ladies but at the time we were both oblivious to this fact. Neither of us were wearing a watch so we innocently asked a passing lady the time.

"Do you want business?" Was her immediate reply.

In our naivety we didn't really know what she meant so she had to spell it out for us. In those days I didn't have a penny to scratch my arse with but my mate had a little bit put away and he very kindly agreed to pay for us both. The three of us walked to a cash machine and then jumped into a taxi. After a short drive she asked the driver to pull up next to some housing estate and then she asked us for the money upfront because she '*needed something from her mates.*' Being the foolish little boys that we were we gave her the money and then watched her leave the car and disappear into the estate. We sat patiently for ten minutes, then the driver spoke up,

"She's not coming back lads, you shouldn't have gave her the money upfront."

We both sat there heartbroken, two little virgins about to have sex for the very first time and now it was gone! The driver saw the disappointment on our faces, he said he'd take us to find some decent girls. It didn't take him long to find two girls stood together

and he knew them both by name, the dirty bastard. We ended up in a back alley, either side of a large bin. I stood with my trousers around my ankles with my cold, little virgin knob hanging out. I was nervous dear reader, she shook it, slapped it but nothing happened. After a couple of minutes she stopped and said,
"I can't do anything with that!"
My mate had no such problems though, this good little Catholic boy lost his virginity with a whore behind a bin in a back alley! At college on the Monday morning, he walked around looking like a ghost. I was never allowed to tell anyone what we'd done. So that was my first experience, being robbed by one and completely failing with the other.

It wasn't until the age of eighteen, in the year 1999, that I would actually have sex with a hooker. By then I wasn't a virgin anymore and had earned a few notches on the bedpost. My first time happened on my first ever night out with my older brother. Our parents were on holiday at the time and at his suggestion we took a couple back the house. Mine was in her forties, she knew it was my first time with a lady like her so she ended up being quite nice to me. She even pretended to enjoy it. When I sit and think about it my big brother has got a lot to answer for. I don't know whether I should thank him or hit him.

The only other girl I can remember from that period was a girl who turned out to be seven months pregnant! When she was stood on the street you honestly couldn't tell. I still managed to do it though. As the millennium rapidly approached and my tastes for drugs grew, my addiction to whores would go to another level.

3
A SOCIALISTS GUIDE TO MARIJUANA

My early adult years were entirely based on getting fucked (I think it's the same for all of us). I'd leave the house on Friday night and come back Sunday tea time. Booze, blow, coke, pills, acid, mushrooms… whatever I could get my hands on. When I think back now to some of the places I ended up in and some of the people I associated with it makes my skin crawl! All of us start drinking in our early teens, some of us sample drugs, some get straight into drugs but whatever our choices are, it's the same for us all, it's about escaping reality.

The first time I smoked cannabis I was either thirteen of fourteen, it wouldn't be until I was seventeen that it became a regular thing. Each day at work was spent just clock watching and waiting for the night to come. A couple of cars of lads, parked in a car park getting stoned. Sat there giggling like a pack of tits and then going home to stuff your face with food. After that I would lay on my bed and listen to Pink Floyd, thinking that somehow the music was changing my life!

I hated work straight away and it wouldn't be until I eventually had my kids that I finally accepted that it's just something everyone has to do in life. In those early years I was a militant little bastard! I was in constant trouble on every job I went on and then eventually you realise you aren't doing yourself any favours and none of the spineless cunts you work with are ever going to back you up. I grudgingly came to accept that management are always going to be hypocrites and that you're never going to beat them.

Everyone has a moment or moments in their lives that either changes them or changes the way they think. At the age of eighteen I was to have one such moment. I was at a house party that my aunty was throwing and the house was rammed with people. I had walked into the front room and I saw a large bald headed man sat down rolling up a spliff. I immediately sat next to him and got chatting to him. My parents were also in the front room, dear reader they are the two most straight laced and sensible people that you could ever wish to meet. My parents both knew by now that I smoked cannabis but I would never be disrespectful enough to sit and smoke it in front of them. So I sat with this man and talked with him whilst he got stoned. At one point in the conversation he asked me,

"Do you read books son?"

"Aye" I replied.

"I want you to promise to read a book for me. It's called The Ragged Trousered Philanthropists."

I can't say that the title sounded very appealing and this stranger wouldn't even tell me what the book was about but I made him a promise anyway. I kept this promise a year later and at the age of nineteen I read the book. Dear reader, if you have never read this book then I urge you to please seek it out. Every single working man in Britain today should read it. It instantly became the best book that I had ever read and it still is today. I can make a bold claim and say it's even better than anything George Orwell ever wrote.

The only problem with reading this book at that age was that it turned an angry young man into an even angrier young man. I became a socialist over night, I rebelled at work, I grew to hate modern society and I just pretty much hated everything. Everything apart from getting fucked. There was a time when I could smoke a spliff as easily as I could smoke a cigarette, nowadays if I even caught a quick whiff of one I would turn into a paranoid wreck. I can say with all honesty that, although I don't regret my days of drugs, they do completely fuck your head. Anyone who denies this or argues against it is talking out of their bellend. Drugs fuck your brain!

My friends and I would hate going to work each day, we looked forward to getting stoned each night but it was the cannabis itself that makes you hate your job even more. It’s a depressant. Then you start taking ecstasy and it becomes that you only live for the weekend! Those Monday mornings became so unbearable I pretty much just started a four day week. I became known as the big dipper at work!

Anyway the mixture of having a head fucked by drugs, a militant attitude and a socialist view of life ended up setting me back. It set me back a long time. I had my first child at the age of 27 and it literally wasn’t till then that I realised what a cunt I actually was. From that point onwards I became a capitalist and I settled down at work. Socialism is good on paper but unfortunately it completely goes against human nature. Capitalism reaches out to our greed and I have come to realise dear reader, that this world is full of horrible greedy men.

4
AUTISTIC BASTARD!

In my short time on this Earth so far, I have never met a 'normal' person. That's because there is no such thing as a 'normal' person, we are all weird in our own little ways. If there's anyone who wants to dispute this fact by screaming out "I'm normal!" I can guarantee you now brother, you will be even weirder than the rest of us. I admit to you that I'm probably a little bit stranger than most people. If you get called weird your entire life then there comes a time when you just have to accept it.

When I was very young my mother knew I wasn't '*quite right*' so she took me to a doctor who misdiagnosed me with having a mild form of dyslexia. I can read and write better than most people I associate with and all my GCSE's were C-grade. My mother's side of the family is huge and in recent years a lot of my young cousins have been diagnosed with having Asperger's (a form of autism), when I was young this was unheard of. A handful of years ago my mam said to me,

"I think you've got a little dose of that Asperger's."

To me it would explain a lot and I imagine that the people who know me have just read that and said to themselves, '*so that's what it is'*. Once I knew this, it became a good excuse to blame all the irrational behaviour in my life on Asperger's. When I was married and my wife would nag me about never visiting her family or getting into trouble at work all the time, I would simply reply,

"Asperger's!"

It's the truth dear reader, my mind doesn't seem to work like other peoples all the time. What bothers most people never seems to bother me (that's how I've gained a reputation of being laid back), on the other hand I get bothered about tiny little things that nobody else would even think about. You'll soon realise that in this book.

I can honestly say that I'm really glad that I've got my 'little dose' of autism, it's made me the person that I am today. People remember people who are a bit different, we call them characters. It must be boring to be completely forgettable. It's been my strange little brain telling me to do stupid things in my life that's allowed me to write this book. It just so happens that drugs and alcohol don't seem to mix very well with autism. Can you imagine Dustin Hoffman's Rain Man after a bottle of whisky?

I've always been one of those people who wanders off from the group on a night out. I used to enjoy getting wrecked with my mates and then I would hit a point where my eyes would glaze over. That would be my cue to leave and have my own little personal adventure. The next day I would have to recount my antics of the night before to my mates on the phone. I always seemed to have a story to tell. Between the ages of 15 and 22 I did so many fucking ridiculous things that I'm lucky to be alive.

5
IT'S A CONTRACTORS LIFE FOR ME

The life of a contractor will seem completely alien to the majority of society, we are the modern day hunter gatherers. We live a life that has absolutely no job security, no pension and we must be willing to travel *anywhere* to work. Some men will stay in their own country, some men will work abroad and most of us will do a mix of both.

It doesn't take long for us to be conditioned into this lifestyle. We have no loyalty to employers, as they use us then in turn we will use them. The idea of spending your entire life working in one place makes our skin crawl. There are some of us who will crave some sort of security and they will choose to stay in the 'lesser' jobs being treated like animals. The rest of us however will scour the land looking for the highest paid job.

To a contractor any job lasting more than six months is classed as a long job and a very long job would be two to three years but never any longer than that. My own personal record at the time of writing is nineteen months (not including my apprenticeship). I would imagine that your average Joe would find that to be an absolutely terrifying thought but to us it's just normal life. Like I said before we are conditioned to it.

The first two years of my apprenticeship were spent in a local training school, after that I had to pack my bags and leave home. I couldn't drive at the time so I had to get trains to different parts of the country that I had never been to before. My first day on site would be spent trying to find a lift and also trying to find out where some decent digs were. I would never be on one site longer than three months so this became a ritual I quickly had to adapt to. It wouldn't be until the age of 22 that I would finally have a driving license.

You have to learn and adapt very quickly. Don't get settled in a job and get used to the fact that you aren't going to like some of the men you're going to have to work alongside. What starts out as frustrating will soon become the norm and eventually you realise that you don't like spending too long on one particular job.

The contractor workforce can be split into two groups, the snivelling cunts and the men who just really don't want to be at work. (These days I work offshore and I've grown to really appreciate my job but all my years onshore I fucking hated it) We have a tradition where if a co-worker dies then everyone leaves site for the afternoon as a mark of respect. A few years ago I was on a large site with over 1100 men working on it. Someone seemed to die nearly every month, though the deaths were never work related. Most men on the site were travelling men so every time a person died we would all go and have the afternoon in the pub. I can remember one morning the man who I was paired up with told me somebody else had died. The look on his face wasn't one of compassion for the man or his family, it was a look that said, *'I'll be in the pub soon'.* A couple of hours of gossip passed and then I'd heard that the rumour had been started by some bloke with a dark sense of humour. When I told my colleague that the rumour was just a wind up his face completely dropped! He actually looked heartbroken...that's how much some men hate their jobs!

There are some people in England who will never get to know what their own regional accent sounds like, to them they just sound 'normal'. When you work away from home you finally discover how you actually talk. I was dismayed to find out that everyone in England thinks Teessider's sound like Geordie's! I can assure you now that we fucking don't, but to the untrained ear I will admit there are some very minor similarities. Obviously you get hear everyone else's accents as well. I have a soft spot for the Brummie accent, to me they just sound like cartoon characters. The Scouser's sound like a Mancunian receiving an electric shock and the stupidest accent I've ever heard is the Carlisle accent. These people sound like the offspring of Geordies who've been raped by goats!

When you work with other men from all around the country you quickly realise that we're all pretty much the same…that is until you hit the north/south divide. This is the point where sense of humour will completely change. Whereas we Northerners are a funny breed, the Southerners wouldn't know a good joke if it punched them in the face. Northern humour is dry and witty and Southern humour consists of talking about yourself a little bit louder and throwing in some swearwords. I've found that I like Southerners best when they try not to make anyone laugh.

Thousands of men suddenly become a very small community. When starting on a new job it is likely that you will know people, no matter whereabouts in the country you are. If you don't know anyone then you are guaranteed to meet people who knows someone that you know.

So why do we choose to stay in this profession? Money (we always laugh when we see university trained people settling for a shitty 30 grand a year job) and also we have a freedom that most people will never experience… but it comes at a very high price. The lack of job security can grind you down, the seasonal nature of our work means our lives can be 'feast or famine' and the lifestyle puts a strain on any marriage. Most contractors are divorced, myself included. As Joe Fagin once sang, '*That's living alright!*'

6
I SAW A FUNNY THING ONE DAY

I don't know how well this story is going to translate on paper but I promise you now, if you had been there at the time you would've laughed as much as I did. We all have memories that make us chuckle and this daft little one seems to tickle me more than most. If I'm lucky enough to have a deathbed in the very distant future then I want this to be the last thing I remember, just so I can go out with a smile on my face.

Every group of lads are similar I think and there always seems to be at least one absolute idiot within the group. It's the mate who is thicker than the rest of you and can't help saying the most idiotic of things. Now I really believe that my old stupid mate is stupider than your stupid mate. He's one of the thickest people that I have ever met. It used to be impossible to watch a film with him, like a child he would constantly ask questions about what was going on, all the way through. He seemed to crash his car every other month. I remember being in his passenger seat one day and he was heading straight for the curb.

When I realised he wasn't planning on swerving out of the way I shouted out at him. When I had looked at him he hadn't been watching the road at all, he had been staring blankly at his car radio, completely in his own little world. I have to admit that's he's a very nice lad and also he's very funny but I think we have these people in our group to make the rest of us feel better about ourselves.

So there was one day when a few of us were stood under a tree, smoking and chatting. At one point my thick friend was holding court, making us all laugh. The tree above us was only small and one of the lower branches was passing just behind the back of his head. As he was talking he had his left hand raised up to this branch and he was holding onto a leaf. He was using his thumb to rub this leaf in a circular motion. (Are you picturing this in your head?) As he was babbling his shite I noticed his hand and what it was doing. I could see that it wasn't a leaf he was holding and rubbing but I wasn't quite sure what it was. I got his attention,

"What the fucks that in your hand?"

He stopped talking and looked at his hand, we were all looking at his hand and by now we could all see what it was that he had been rubbing so affectionately with his thumb. It was a used condom that some dirty bastard had tied to the branch. There was a moment or two when we all just stared, he didn't let go straight away, his thick brain took a second or two to compute. When he did realise his face was overcome by a look of disbelief and he snapped his hand back as if a shark had just went for it. Screaming out,

"I thought it was a fucking leaf!"

Dear reader, I laughed until I had floods of tears running down my face. It could only of happened to him.

7
IF EASILY OFFENDED PLEASE SKIP

In this chapter I'm going to tell you a joke but before I do there's quite a few points that we are going to have to clear up first. I want to say from the outset that I am not a joke type of person, in fact I'd go as far to say that I really don't like jokes. They very rarely make me laugh and I can't stand those blokes who walk around with a joke book implanted in their brains. Why is it that these men always have creepy stares? After telling you their shit joke they will stand and stare at you, without blinking, waiting until they get some sort of reaction. At this stage in my life I have very little patience with anyone and when I come across these clowns I will tell them straight away,

"I don't like jokes mate."

When they have finished their embarrassing words and the creepy stare kicks in, I will simply reply,

"Like I said mate, I don't like jokes."

My days of humouring people are over, but after saying all this I am about to tell you a joke. There are reasons for this of course, main one being I have never got tired of this joke. Also only one person has ever told me this joke in my entire life, it's not very popular so I believe that you deserve to hear it. The reason its unpopular isn't because its shit, it's because it's so offensive, on so many different levels, that not many people dare to tell it. If you work in construction and you've already heard this joke there is a real chance that it stems from me telling it to someone somewhere down the line. I heard it when I was about 15/16 and I've told it to a lot of people over the last seventeen years. Never once hearing it told back to me and never once meeting a person who's heard it before.

My next point is I genuinely am not a racist person and laughing at a racist joke doesn't make a person racist either. I could sit on a train and quite happily talk to anyone sat next to me, no matter where they were from in the world. (Admittedly I wouldn't be too happy about sitting next to a Paki with a bomb strapped to him of course). If you are reading this and you are of colour and you don't like your brethren being mocked, then please do as the title says and skip.

My next point is I don't like these easily offended, complaining types. The sort of people who write to newspapers and TV stations with letters of complaint. Now I can't imagine someone like that reading this book in the first place but if you think you fit this description then please… just fuck off! I'm not interested in your whining's and nobody else is interested in your whining's either. Why can't you just get a proper hobby?!

My last point is my most crucial. A joke is just a joke. People these days are so obsessed with not offending others that they forget that we are all offended by different things. What offends me might not offend anybody else. It's impossible to make everybody happy, so what is the point in even beginning to try? Let's all forget about it and embrace being offended, then everyone won't be so scared of speaking their minds anymore. As one Australian comedian once said,

"Who cares about being offended? Nothing actually happens to you."

So what follows is just a joke, if you don't like it then don't worry, your life isn't going to change. If you do like it then please don't be scared to tell it, people will either laugh or they will shake their heads in disgust.

Remember I didn't make this joke up and the days of shooting the messenger are in the past. So after that quite massive build-up, here it is.

THE MRS'S JONES JOKE

Mrs. Jones is in the hospital after just giving birth to a baby. The doctor comes in and says,

DOCTOR- "Mrs Jones, I've got some good news and some bad news."

MRS. JONES- "What's the bad news Doctor?"

DOCTOR- "Mrs Jones, your baby is black and has ginger hair!"

MRS. JONES- "Oh my word! What's the good news?"

DOCTOR- "It's dead."

8
I HATE EVERYTHING!
PART ONE

Welcome to part one of my ‘I Hate Everything’ chapters. I detest a lot of things in life dear reader and if I sat down and thought about them all this book would be ten times longer. I’ve got a long enough list for now though and I’ve made the decision to split it into three chapters because I’m pretty sure if you read them all in one go your eyeballs would start to itch.

Unlike the rest of the chapters in this book these chapters have no chronological order. They can be thrown into parts one, two or three it doesn’t really matter. They are just a series of rants that I feel like getting off my chest. If you find yourself agreeing with me then you are truly wiser than you could ever have first imagined.

CONSTRUCTION WORKERS- I’m picking on construction workers here because that’s the industry that I work in, but I realise that people will be the same no matter what their profession, so really this is just about everyone.

In school a kid who tells tales on his/her classmates to the teacher is called the school sprag or grass. When they grow up these kids don't change and as they become adults they will sprag on their workmates to the boss. The unfortunate thing is, money makes nice people do horrible things and you soon realise that there are a lot more of these spragger's and grasses than you could ever have first imagined. I work in a male dominated environment and I have come to learn that men gossip as much, if not more, than women. It's a fact that I have come to grudgingly accept, I think it's just human nature. When I'm in a short term job it's easy for me to just pass through without getting involved in these shenanigans. In longer jobs it's a lot harder not to get involved. If I learn that someone has been gossiping about me then I'm the type of man who is happy to confront them about it, but as time passes I find it becomes inevitable that I will start to gossip about that particular person as well. (Which makes me just as bad as them). What I really can't stand though, and I will never get used to, is when the gossip leaves the shop floor and enters management's office. In my industry we don't call these men sprag's or grasses, we call them WRETCHES!

There are three types of wretch in life, dear reader. The first type of wretch is your management wretch. This is a man who could put someone's father out of a job as easily as he could flick a light switch. These men have absolutely no morals in life and all they care about is their bonus.

The second type of wretch is a man who works on the tools but has ambition to climb the ladder. In construction it's rare for a man to be promoted to foreman by merit. It does happen but it's a lot more common for a man to climb the ladder by stabbing his workmates in the back. These men always have two things in common, they tend to be absolute lazy cunts and they will also always deny having any ambition to climb the ladder. More often than not these men slag off the management more than anyone else. These men are natural born liars and they will tell lies about their workmates just to cover their own backs.

The third type of wretch is easily the worst of all and these are the most common type of wretch that there is, in fact it's frightening and sad at just how many of these wretches exist. These are the men who have no ambition to climb the ladder but they want to hang onto their jobs for as long as possible. The first thing these men do is get friendly with as many gaffers as possible, some of them will even go so far as changing their local pub to their gaffers local or taking up golf! From here they move onto slagging off as many of their workmates as they can manage. It's something that they do all day long with as many of the management who care to listen. In return for their brilliant backstabbing ability, any lack of ability to actually do their job is overlooked and they will be rewarded by always being first and last on the job. The worst thing is a lot of these men come across as the nicest people that you could ever wish to meet. You know that at home they will be decent family men and their friends will comment on how nice they are. Then they go to work and turn into the most morally corrupt bastards that you could ever have the misfortune of meeting.

The statement I'm about to make I mean with all sincerity. I hope every single wretch has a horrific accident which puts them into a mobility scooter for the rest of their lives! They have ruined every single job that I have ever been on!

MINGEBAGS- Mingebag is a word used to describe a 'tight-fisted' person. I don't know why I let these people bother me because if being tight with their money is what makes these people happy then I should just accept it. I think it's a waste of a life though, we are all only here once, so why not just enjoy your life? These idiots will work every single hour of their life available to them. They will go through life refusing to spend a penny, when it comes to retirement age they will carry on working, still grabbing every hour that they can. Then they're in a box six feet under and their family will be spending all the money that they refused to spend. What was the point in that? They missed out on everything in life and they never created a single decent memory!

A man once told me about a notorious mingebag that he had worked with. They had been sat on their break on a Friday nightshift and this mingebag was sat talking on his phone.

"Sorry I can't be there sweetheart, I couldn't get out of work. Have a lovely night though."

The man asked the mingebag who he had been talking to and the mingebag replied,

"My daughter, she's having her 18th birthday party."

There was only one problem with this though, at that company Friday night was purely overtime, it wasn't part of his contracted hours! The horrible cunt!

There's also funny stories about mingebag's and this one has always stuck in my mind. Four men were travelling down south from Teesside in a car, they were on their way to start a new job. Again one of these men is a notorious mingebag. They stopped at a motorway café to get their breakfast and this café has a help yourself counter. The three normal men sit down with their full English breakfasts and the mingebag sits down with a bowl of soup, a bun and a fork. One of the men pointed out to the mingebag that he'd picked up a fork instead of a spoon and the mingebag replied,

"Why do I need a spoon?"

He then proceeded to stab his fork into his soup and produced four sausages from the bowl, which he then placed into his bun! The tight bastard!

Like I said before, if working every moment of their life and not spending any money is what makes them happy then just let them get on with it. I just don't understand the point in them living.

CAT OWNERS- There was a time, not that long ago, when I used to hate cats with a burning passion. When I was married my front and back gardens were my pride and joy, I had spent a lot of time and money on them. It took time to attract wild birds to my garden and when they did finally arrive it was short lived. Two blackbirds were torn to pieces within the space of a month, after that birds rarely visited. The final straw for me came when I had just bought one of those expensive leaf blowers. I was in my front garden giving my new toy its *very* first go and I had it set on 'suck'. Halfway through sucking up a large pile of leaves that had gathered on my driveway, I was struck by the strongest smell of cat shit that I have ever encountered in my life! The leaf blower had sucked up a cat turd, shredded it and then spattered it into the collection bag! I had to immediately clean my brand new toy, shouting and swearing to myself as I did. When I finished I went onto the internet and googled the words 'how to poison a cat?' I then drove to my nearest supermarket and purchased two items, cat food and car engine coolant. (The till worker gave me a dirty look by the way) When I got home I was all set to mix the ingredients when my stupid wife talked me out of it. She told me that I could be killing a child's pet. One of the saddest days of my life was at the age of 10 when my dog was ran over and killed. Her mental blackmail worked and the lethal ingredients were stored away.

These days I don't hate cats anymore, they're just a species of animal doing what comes naturally to them. I do however hate their human owners and the biased laws in this country! Why is a dog owner fined for public shitting but not the cat owner? (By that I mean the dog shitting, not the human owner) Cat owners are all lazy bastards who only picked a cat as a pet because they're too fucking bone idle to look after a real pet! They always have the same excuse,

"Cats can't be domesticated." Fucking bullshit!

A man once pointed out to me that you will never see a Persian cat walking the streets. This is because the cat would be immediately stolen and sold. Out of fear of this happening the owners keep the cats indoors and DOMESTICATE them. There you go, no more bullshit excuses! If you can't be arsed looking after a pet then don't have one, you fucking slobs!

BIG MEN- As far as I'm concerned big men are all the same, they all have three things in common. When they stand in a pub they give it the 'big I am'. They all want to be noticed by us smaller men and they expect us to be wary of them. Dear reader, it's a false image because their work life and home life are a far cry from the 'big I am' that they pretend to be in the pub.

Big men seem to fall in love exceedingly easily. They are that soppy that they will propose to their new girlfriends in a matter of months, if not weeks! When they do get married these men will always be completely mothered by their wives, like the big babies that they really are. (They're always mammies' boys as well by the way).

When they're at work they tend to be the biggest cocksuckers on the job. They keep up the 'big man' image in the locker room but in the offices they will always tip their cap to the management and belly laugh at the gaffers shit jokes.

Big men you are nothing more than molly coddled, emotionally insecure cocksuckers!

GHOULISH MEERKATS- This is a term coined by the comedian Charlie Brooker, he uses it to describe those sick bastards that stand and stare at accidents. I wish I could've thought of it myself because it truly is the best description for these twisted perverts. The amount of my life that has been wasted in traffic jams caused by ghoulish meerkats is unbelievable! I'll never get that time back. I've lost it because nosey, sick cunts have slammed on their brakes to look at an accident in the opposite lane. I could've been at home masturbating with that precious time.

I remember once being on a 40 mph road in Stockton-on-Tees. At the side of the road a man was being arrested by two policeman. It was happening right at the side of the road, anyone could've just had a quick glance and carried on without slowing down. Unfortunately I found myself driving at a snail's pace and then I came to an abrupt stop. The reason I had to stop was because the car in front of me had crashed into the car in front of him. There were two reasons the man crashed his car, one he was looking at the police instead of the road and the main reason was because the car in front of him had actually stopped dead in the middle of the road! A 40 mph road and this ghoulish meerkat had stopped his car dead! What's wrong with these fucking people? I did quite a bit of shouting when I managed to get past.

The worst personal example I have happened when I was about 16. I was sat on a bus which had pulled up to a junction, just before it managed to pull out a car smashed into the front of it. We all had to get off the bus and as I walked past the car I took a glance. Every window in it was smashed and sat on the back seat was a young girl screaming at the top of her lungs. It sent a shiver down my spine. I saw people were helping so I carried on walking and turned away from the horrific sight but not everyone did the same as me. Surrounding the car was a crowd of people, they were standing staring, not speaking and not helping. These are the true ghoulish Meerkats. Why anyone would want to stand at stare at distressed young girl is completely beyond me.

I actually talked about this subject with some workmates and it was made clear to me that I was the weird one for not staring. Dear reader, sometimes I fucking hate the human species!

GYPO'S- It seems that these days we aren't allowed to use words that we've spent our entire lives saying anymore. Apparently a Greasy Wop is now called an Italian and a filthy scumbag gypsy is called a Traveller! Its political correctness gone mad! Fortunately there are still some of us who don't give a fuck what the PC brigade say. A filthy gypsy will always be a gypo to me.

In life it is always wrong to stereotype people. People should never be judged by their race or gender…but we have one exception to the rule and that's the fucking gypo's! These people are without a doubt the biggest scumbags on the planet! Their whole life is based on fighting, causing havoc, exploiting the elderly, theft and draining public resources.

I'm lucky that I have only ever had to endure one episode of that horseshit 'Big Fat Gypsy Wedding'. Due to this series the uneducated do-gooders of England have now started sticking up for this bunch of hooligans. There was a documentary about gypsies on TV last year that I missed but apparently it had all the do-gooders up in arms. Why you ask? Because it showed gypsies committing crimes and being thugs. The do-gooders said it was anti-traveller propaganda, in response the documentary maker said, 'I just filmed what I saw.'

How is it we all have to pay income tax, council tax and national insurance but this lot doesn't? Why are they allowed to use our schools, use our hospitals, claim benefits and claim pensions? These people are the cancer of the country, they don't contribute anything at all to society! All they do is bring misery to the normal people who they harass and rob on an everyday basis.

Gypsies fuck off back to Ireland and Romania and please, please stop breeding! (Lucky for me that none those thick pikey's can read!)

LAUNDRETTES- What are laundrettes for? Don't worry dear reader, I'm not thick, I know what they're for but why do they exist in modern day England? In a society where everyone owns everything 'on tick' why don't some people have a fucking washing machine?

I could go onto any council estate in England and find lots of houses that are kitted out a lot more expensively than my own. Some of these houses will have been done up with cash but the majority of them will be done up on finance. (In fact most privately owned houses are done up on finance as well). There will be houses in this country where the people occupying them don't work but they will have *'paid'* £100 per spindle on their fucking staircase! It's ridiculous and it's also stupid but that's just modern society. So back to the question, if this is the world we live in now, why are there people who still refuse to pay for a washing machine?

I'm the type of man who begrudges having to go shopping, I can't stand going to the barbers and I really couldn't think of anything worse than carrying my soiled undies to a shop and sit waiting for an hour for them to clean and dry! Some people might say to me,

"For some people it's just a way of getting out of the house and socialising"

My reply to that would be,

"Are you taking the fucking piss?!"

Surely a tiny boxed in shop with constant loud machines running all day is the worst place for people to socialise? And surely your average human being would rather sit in the house than in that environment? I really don't understand these people. I've never been in a laundrette in my life but I've walked past a few and I get a shudder every time I look through the window. There's no excuse for them!

PRIDE PARADES- I'm white and I'm heterosexual. (Although those of you who've read the ladyboy chapter in my first book may disagree with that last bit) These are two things that I never think about and I couldn't care less about. There are some people who feel the need to scream at the top of their lungs and shout about how proud they are of their sexuality, their race, their religion. Now I don't really care that these people feel the need to do that. A thousand gays mincing down a street doesn't bother me. BUT if we go back to my first line of this chapter, could I stick the words "I'm proud that" in front of that sentence? The truth is I don't think I'd be allowed to.

"I'm proud that I'm white and heterosexual" I think if I stood in a street and shouted that, I would be arrested and deemed a racist. Like I said at the start, I don't give a fuck about being white or heterosexual, but I can't stand hypocrisy! If black people can scream it in the street then why can't I? No matter what the do-gooders say about 'multicultural' England the fact is England is a white, heterosexual country. Anyone who is stupid enough to argue with me on that point then don't worry, I've got plenty of evidence to back my claim up. It seems these days that if you're part of the majority then you're the enemy! When did we become the enemy? The gays need to thank their heterosexual parents for creating them and the ethnic minorities need to thank the whites for creating a nice country for them to live in. I might see if I can get all these gays and ethnic minorities together and see if they'll have a *'Thank*

You White, Heterosexual Man Parade' I can't see it happening though.

Pride parades don't bother me unless I know for certain that ANYONE can have them… and right now I don't believe that to be the case at all.

PART TWO

THE NOUGHTIES

9
TRICKED BY A MIDGET

For my nineteenth birthday party in the year 2000, I threw a house party that has gone down in legend within my social group. By that age I was living in a decent sized four bed detached house. My parents were on holiday and my older brother had moved out.

A total of 48 people passed through my mam and dads house that night and I'll admit that I didn't know a good chunk of them, they were friends of friends. In the large dining room we had decks and a strobe light set up, the adjoining kitchen was where people were trying to escape the noise of the music a little bit and the front room was full of people chilling out and getting stoned. It was a party I'm still proud of. The next day the house was in ruin and it took some hours graft to tidy it. I also had to repair the front room carpet as there was four large rock-fall burns in it. If my own kids ever attempt to have a party like that in my house one day, I'll write them out of my will!

Whilst the party was in full swing I had gone into the front room at one point and saw a girl perched on the edge of my settee. I didn't know her or her three mates but apparently they had all gone to school with one of my good mates. I had a brief chat with this girl but she didn't stay at the party for long. About a week later my mate rang me and told me that this girl wanted to meet me. I took the invitation and saw her a week later at my mates house. There were five of my mates and her, she was the only girl. We sat in the kitchen separate from everyone for an hour or so and then joined everyone else in the front room. When she sat down on the settee next to me I noticed that her legs didn't leave the edge and also the heels on her shoes were huge! I couldn't help but ask how tall she was. 4'9"! I didn't believe her at first so I asked her to take her shoes off and stand next to me. Sure enough it was like standing next to a kid, she then admitted that the heels of her shoes were 5" high! I don't know what constitutes a midget but she can't have been far off, although she was all in proportion.

I think at that age we are all at our most shallow and I'll admit that her height did make me feel a bit queasy and completely put me off her. Having said that it didn't take long for us to go upstairs and start shagging in my mates bed. She turned out to be the best shag I'd had in my life so far. When she was riding me she was perched on her little feet, it was class! Later on in the night we went back up for round two.

After that night she wanted to meet again. Her height embarrassed me but her skill in the bedroom made up for it, so I met her for what would turn out to be the last time. This time it was around her parent's house, they were away and her friends were there. I was the only person smoking blow. Dear reader, I've never felt so out of place in my life. Her friends were all boring cunts and very weirdly one of them was her ex-boyfriend who was about 4" taller than me! They must have looked a right strange couple!

One thing I'll always remember from that night was her twin sister. They weren't identical but they were the same height and her sister was chubby. She was sat on the floor in the middle of the room, with her short legs sort of crossed and at one point she got excited about something and started clapping her chubby little hands together. I can remember staring at her and feeling physically sick!

I barely spoke a word to anyone, I was sat smoking spliff after spliff and also drinking cans to try and take the edge of the situation. I never relaxed all night and when we finally went up to the bedroom it was a relief. We shagged and then I tried to sleep. The mixture of blow, alcohol and exercise had started making my head spin. I laid there trying to ignore it but then the moment came, I sat up and projectile vomited all over her carpet and the end of her quilt. She helped me stumble to the shower, naked and covered in my own sick. When I was brave enough to go back in the bedroom she was on her knees cleaning up the last of my carrots out of the carpet. I got back into bed and passed out.

When I woke the next day I apologised. She dropped me off at home and when we pulled up outside my house she simply said,

"See you later."

It was the best possible outcome really. Dear reader, I promise you now that that's the only time in my life that I have been sick all over a midget's bedroom.

10
THE CRACKWHORE AND THE CLAP

When I was nineteen I went out one Friday night and got pilled up. Ecstasy was my drug of choice in those days and my friends and I were bang into the clubbing scene. I'm pretty sure that I have never pulled a girl whilst being on ecstasy, I was always more interested in dancing my tits off. It would be once I'd left a club and the drugs would start to wear off when I would be overcome by sexual urges. This mixture of being stood in the street in the early hours, horny as fuck and a knowledge of the red light district is when my love for prostitutes truly blossomed. Of all the stories of encounters with prostitutes that you are going to read, this is the one that sticks in my head the most.

So we had all went out this particular night and after the club there was no house party for us to go back to. I did my usual and sloped off from the group. I jumped in a taxi and before too long I had picked up a half-cast girl (or mixed race if that makes you happier). We went back to her flat in the centre of town and on route she rang a drug dealer. When I walked into the flat there was a big ginger bloke sparked out on the settee, wearing only his boxer shorts. Almost immediately there was a knock on the door, it was her rock of crack being delivered, which I had to pay for.

We sat in the front room and I smoked crack for the first time in my life. (Anyone getting worried that I'm some sort of scumbag then please don't, I've only done it a handful of times). Like any other drug the first time is the best, I had a hit and completely sank back into my seat. I can remember that she turned on the telly and there was some cartoons on. What a fucking surreal memory that is for me, watching cartoons and smoking crack with a prostitute whilst some big, semi-naked twat was laid fast asleep a few feet away from me. He never stirred the whole time I was there.

By the time we went into the bedroom it was daylight outside and all the crack had been smoked. I laid on the bed and received quite a magnificent blowjob. Because of all the drugs in my system it took me ages to cum, luckily she wasn't the rush type. She was persistent and didn't give up until she had seen the job through. I got a taxi home with a smile on my face. This was the Saturday morning.

At that point in my life I was working in Tipton near Birmingham. I got back down there the Sunday night, ready to start work the Monday morning. On the Monday night I went to the toilet in my digs for a piss. (This is the point in the story where a lot of men are going to get worried.) When I took my tiddle out, I had snot peeping out of my foreskin. Yes dear reader, it was gonorrhoea and yes, you can catch it from a blowjob, it infects the throat as well as the quim!

As I was away from home I just had to put up with it for the week but day by day it got worse and worse. You will hear men say that it's like pissing razor blades, the best description, I think, is it's more like pissing boiling water. It really, really hurts. On the Thursday night I was to do something incredibly stupid. I got pissed up and decided that I couldn't resist having a wank any longer. Dear reader, I can assure you now that the point of climax was one of the most painful experiences of my life. Easily the most pain my poor little knob has ever been in. I actually yelped out loud like a dog when I came. I wouldn't recommend it to anyone.

What a weekend, two firsts, crack and the clap. We all need to thank the Sweaty Sock who discovered penicillin. As well as saving billions of lives, that man also saved my little tail. I salute you sir!

11
GOING DUTCH

At the age of twenty, myself and two of my best mates set off to Holland to start a new job together. What lay in front of us would turn out to be one of the best times of my life. The job itself would turn out to be a bag of spanners and the money was pretty shit but the digs were second to none and our workmates were all a good bunch of lads.

The digs were on a Dutch holiday camp, a bit of a poorer man's Butlins. There were around 15 of us English lads spread out over 3 massive chalets. In my chalet were my two mates and two other lads of a similar age and we all clicked straight away. I had that job for eight weeks and it turned out to be an eight week party. Magic mushrooms, cocaine, ecstasy, weed and lots of alcohol. The people on the holiday camp absolutely hated us, all except the pub landlord. (He probably did hate us but he loved our money)

We were on an island with no big towns near us, it took about two weeks before I got to experience my first Dutch brothel. Only two of us went and it took about an hour in a taxi. We went to a few pubs before we went to the actual brothel, once in there I was to have my first ever black girl. After I had done the business I waited in the brothel bar for my mate. I was quite inebriated, I bought a drink each for me and the girl and sat down with her. When I sat down I quickly realised just how much I'd paid for the drinks. I can't remember the amount now but I know it was a lot! Being the drunken dick I was I took the drinks back to the bar and demanded my money back. An argument ensued with the bartender and then a man to my right piped up. One minute I was shouting at him and the next I was laid on the floor outside the brothel. When I had come to, there were four men stood over me, they weren't putting the boot in, I think they were just waiting for me to regain consciousness. When I did they all just went back inside leaving me on the floor. I staggered to my feet and then to retain a little bit of dignity I gave the brothel door a good boot before quickly walking to a bar around the corner. I waited in the doorway for my mate to pass, when I saw him we jumped straight into a taxi and headed back to the digs. I sat in the front seat of the taxi and checked my face in the mirror, my head felt a bit tender. There was a crescent moon shaped graze near my temple, whether I was hit with a bottle or a sovereign ring I'm not sure. I deserved it to be honest.

About four weeks into the job it was one of the lads nineteenth birthday party and to celebrate we all went out in Rotterdam. We were taxied there in a minibus by one of the Dutch lads from site. He also provided our cocaine for the evening, which turned out to be rocket fuel. It wasn't normal coke, it was yellow and sticky, I don't know what it was mixed with but it was strong. I can't remember the first hour or so of the night, my eyes must have been in the back of my head. I can't even remember my first prostitute of the night, I just know that she was black and that I didn't cum. We spent the night going from brothel to brothel, that weird coke had been dynamite, no matter how hard I tried I just couldn't cum.

I ended up having another black girl, a white girl and an oriental. The Dutch lad drove us back to the digs and I was sat there feeling really frustrated. I'm sure those brothels cheat with the thirty minutes allotted time! When we got back to the digs only two of us stayed up drinking. At 10am there was a knock on our door. It was two of the older blokes from another room, who hadn't come out with us. They were about to head off to Dan Hague to look at the window prostitutes there, so I decided to go with them. By the time we got there I felt absolutely fucked, my hangover had well and truly kicked in. I had to force myself to go with a girl. Yet again I didn't cum, the con artist wasted most of my half hour on a striptease!

That's my own personal record dear reader. Five prostitutes in less than 24 hours. I will never beat it. I was only 20, no beer gut and pumped full of drugs that gave me stamina and refused to let me cum. (To anyone who's had five girls at once then that's not the same thing, that only counts as one session! OK Jamie?!)

This one big party came literally crashing to an end on my eighth week, after a minor mishap with a forklift truck. When I'd first arrived on site they had asked me if I could drive a forklift, I had told them no but I could learn. They, very illegally, let me loose on them. The forklift trucks they had came in three different sizes, small, medium and fucking massive! I was allowed to drive all three.

The Dutch lads on site used to work a half day on a Friday but the English lads had to do a full day's shift. When the Dutch lads finished the gaffer and his lapdog would sneak into a shed at the back of the site, open up some Heineken and do guvvy jobs. Every Friday afternoon I would wait for all the Dutch to disappear then I'd jump into the smallest forklift and rag it all over the fucking site! One time I very briefly got it onto two wheels without tipping it! I'll come clean, it was a complete accident and I absolutely shit myself!

Those Friday afternoons were destined to end in tragedy and they did. I crashed the little bastard straight into some big fucking machine and on this afternoon the foreman was having a wander, sods law! Due to my militant attitude the gaffer hated me anyway and had been waiting for an excuse to get rid of me. I handed it to him on a plate. I was sacked on the spot and I was heartbroken. (The first time you get sacked isn't a very pleasant experience)

12
PUMPED UP ON MAGIC MONKEY JUICE!

I've stolen that title from a TV comedy series called The Brass Eye, if you've never seen this series then do yourself a favour and watch it. (Make sure you watch the drugs episode first)

Dear reader, for many people the first time they take ecstasy it is the best drug experience that they will ever have. It's quite a special moment. For me though it was a different drug, the most natural drug we have on this planet…magic mushrooms. The first time that I ever sampled this marvellous wonder was during my stint in Holland. They were Mexican mushrooms and on them I had one of the best nights of my life. This particular night only three of us partook in this hallucinogenic delight. We took them in our digs and when they started to 'kick in' we set off on what would become the best adventure that the three of us will probably ever have.

For anyone who doesn't know, Holland and its surrounding islands have dams all along the coast line. The three of us would find ourselves stood on top of one of these dams this night. To one side of the dam was a woodland with old fashioned street lamps and chalets and to the other side was the blackness of the surrounding sea. It's hard to describe a hallucinogenic trip to anyone, regardless of whether a person has had one or not. I'm assuming everybody read the Ladybird books when they were young, all those famous kids fairy tales? The best way to describe this trip, is that it was like we had just walked into one of these books. The lit up woodland became the edges of a magical kingdom and the dark sea became a land where only evil dwelled. Above us the full moon seemed to have six or seven sister moons and the clouds in the sky were passing overhead at bullet speed, constantly changing shape. It was incredible dear reader and I'll never forget it.

The first time that I took our own home grown English mushrooms it was an intense experience. The people I took them with refused to go for a walk and instead we just sat around a campfire in the middle of some woods. It was a battle to keep the paranoia and a bad trip at bay. They were a lot stronger than the Mexican variety, a bit too strong.

There used to be a shop in Middlesbrough town centre that sold legal highs. I don't know if it's still there but it sold all sorts of drug paraphernalia, bongs and such like. To mine and my friend's great delight this shop also sold magic mushrooms. Mushrooms of the Mexican variety. They were able to get away with this because of some loophole in the law which dictated that a mushroom had to be dried out to be deemed illegal. (I can't believe that I live in a country that classes one of its indigenous plants as an illegal substance!) We would frequent this shop for our mushrooms as the Mexican ones were far superior to the English ones.

One night three of my mates and I made a critical error. We decided to make a mushroom broth, only it wasn't a broth it was just boiling water with mushrooms thrown in and nothing else added. We then headed for the North York Moors where we camped for the night. Our site was on top of the Cleveland Hills, we sat around a campfire in our camp chairs overlooking the view of Teesside. It was a spot for Kings. The Magic Broth was contained in a flask and the flask lid became the goblet that we would all share from. I can tell you now dear reader it was the most disgusting fucking thing that I have ever tasted in my life, I don't know what you're supposed to add to it but the very thought of it now is making me feel sick! The Devil's Vomit would be the best description for it.

The four of us managed to have two cups each, it was enough for the trip to start, after that each cup became harder and harder. We all sat there, hallucinating with a horrible taste in our mouths and our guts felt like they were full of petrol. As the vile chalice was passed from person to person it all became a bit too much. We would take a mouthful, force it down, throw it back up, force down another mouthful, throw that back up and then pass the cup along. It's a funny memory now when I think about the four us sat there together, all taking it in turns to be sick to the side of our chairs. Put it this way dear reader, that flask never got finished in the end.

Magic mushrooms! If God existed, they would've of been the best thing he ever invented.

13
CHRIST ON A BIKE

I decided that I was Atheist at the age of 21. Being brought up Catholic I was forced to go to church every Sunday until the age of 16. My parents weren't bible basher's, they were just doing what their parents had done to them. I believed in God until I was around 18, its embarrassing now when I think about it but if a child's mind is polluted from the start then it's hard to reset the brain. From the ages of 18 to 21 I didn't really know what I believed in, I knew that organised religions were all bullshit but I still believed in ghosts and other crackpot musings. In those years I started to educate myself more with books.

There were two books in particular that completely unchained my mind from all the dogshit. The first book explained how the human brain works, did you know that the part of the brain that is active when using your imagination is the same part of the brain that is active when thinking about religion?

The second book was an attack on all organised religion. It was scathing, it was true and it made me realise how deluded I had been. After reading these two books I didn't believe in *anything* anymore.

There's no life after death, there's no such thing as ghosts, we don't have aliens walking amongst us etc. It's all just human imagination. No religion has any shred of evidence to support it, every time science disproves a piece of it then religion bends to suit. Who do we trust more? The most intelligent men of the modern era or the backwards thinking men of 3000 years ago who thought the earth was flat and the sun revolved around it? (I can remember talking to a friend of mine who still believes in God and I told him about these books. He said to me, "So someone writes a book and you believe every word they say?" My reply to that was, "Isn't that what you've done?")

I have only one disagreement with the author of the second book, he believed religion should be eradicated altogether. I believe that people who live in abject poverty, in a country that has absolutely NO chance of ever developing, have the right to a religion. They have a miserable existence, let them believe in a perfect, everlasting life at the end of it.

Dear reader, have you ever sat and thought about that last line before? '*Perfect, everlasting life.*' If you think hard about it you soon realise what complete and utter wank it is. Only a human brain could come up with that shite! In the end we go to a place where everything is perfect, you're always happy, you never get sick and you never die! That's just the complete opposite of real life! Do we hate our lives that much that we want to live the complete opposite of it? I think heaven sounds horrendous, do we really want to spend eternity with all those family members we hate? Why don't we just spend our real lives enjoying it, instead of wasting it on preparation for a life that doesn't even exist?

Religion, like money, is a form of control. These are the two biggest tools in life to control the masses but they are also the two reasons we have war and all hate each other. Coincidence?

Religion is a complete hypocrisy! Christianity teaches us that it's bad to be rich, look at the Pope. Islam teaches us that it's bad to kill people, the Muslims can't have read that bit. Judaism teaches us eye for an eye, well done Israel, you're the only ones who actually practise what you preach and it just so happens that you're the most evil bastards out of the lot!

Dear reader, I hope by now that you have come to trust me? Trust me when I say there is no such thing as heaven, no such thing as hell and no such thing as God. Tell Christ to get on his bike and fuck off!

14
A LOSS OF INNOCENCE IN ONE NIGHT

A few years ago I was having a drink with a friend of mine who's married. He was telling me that he was happy but he lived his life wishing he'd had just one really filthy night like the night I'd had. The night he was talking about is one I'm going to tell you about in this chapter. Call me naïve but I thought every man got to have at least one filthy lass in their life? Maybe I've been lucky because I've had a few. I know that the story that follows will actually seem tame to a lot of men. I don't do scat, I don't do piss, I'm not interested in masks or whips. My friends call me a dirty bastard but in the scheme of things I'm just a bog standard man.

This night happened when I was 21 years old. The dedication at the start of this book is a nod to the girl in the story. After this night I never saw her again but I've never forgotten her name. I was out on the town with a few mates and early in the night I bumped into an old associate that I hadn't seen in a couple of years. He was with people who I didn't know, we had a quick chat and then parted company.

A couple of bars later I saw him again. This time I had one of those once in a lifetime moments that you wish could happen every week but unfortunately never do. He approached me and said,

"See that girl over there?"

He pointed to his group of friends and a half decent looking girl was staring at me.

"Yeah" I replied.

"She wants to fuck you."

I can remember being a bit lost for words for a second.

"But she's hasn't spoken to me."

"I know but I told her you were a dirty bastard."

Dear reader, I couldn't believe my fucking luck. I asked where he was going later and told him I'd meet up with him at the end of the night. I carried on drinking with my mates and I didn't meet up with that girl until all the clubs were closed.

I ended up in some house and me and her went straight upstairs. I went down on her first, her clout was huge! I had my first ever attempt at fisting but I didn't realise at the time that there was a technique to it. I had all my hand in just past the thumb knuckle but then it wouldn't go any further, I was a silly little boy who missed out on a golden opportunity, if only I'd watched more fisting porn at the time! I gave her ring piece a good licking and then got a couple of fingers in there. At one point she was laid on her belly with her arse pointing up, I had four fingers past the knuckles in her twat and then three fingers in her bullet hole at the same time. Next she went down on me, she put a finger up my bum and after a time she tried to put another one up, I told her one was enough. After that some pretty bog standard sex followed.

Have you ever noticed that after shagging a complete stranger how you'll lay and talk about things that you'd never say to anyone else? Well dear reader, I will never forget the things that this girl said to me. It started with her telling me of her love for porn, then she told me that one of her favourite pastimes was cutting a cucumber in half and using it to DP herself! After this the conversation started to get dirty. She admitted to having threesomes with two men, threesomes with a man and woman, I laid there starting to feel like a shy little virgin. Then she told me her ultimate fantasy… when she finished I laid there in stunned silence. I can't remember now how long I was quiet for or what I finally replied with but she had just told me that she fantasised about being raped!

When it came to round two she asked me to be rough. This time I bent her over and just put it straight up her arse. She told me to spank her hard so I did, I slapped her arse has hard as I could. She got quite a shock, it actually hurt my hand. I gave her few good smacks and then pushed her face into the pillow, holding it down with as much force as possible. I'm going to be honest dear reader, I didn't feel comfortable doing any of it. If I met her today I'm pretty sure I'd leave her black and blue.

After cumming all over her face we went to sleep. When I woke up the next morning I quickly shagged her up the arse again and then got a taxi home. I never saw her or that old associate again. That was the first proper dirty girl of my life.

15
PROSTITUTES PART TWO THE FINAL YEARS

From the ages of twenty to twenty-two my life was a sleazefest, I had mucky holidays in the sun, filthy one night stands and lots and lots of prostitutes! I fucked those whores in all sorts of places, back alleys, crack-den toilets, my parent's house and even a school playground! (Don't worry it was 04:00 in the morning and on a weekend) There is one place that brings a smile to my face though. Any readers from Teesside will well be aware of the Hotel F1 on Portrack Lane. I don't know what it's called these days but when it was the F1 it was basically just a knocking shop. I think a room there cost about £17.50 a night when I was that age. I only ever used it twice! My first encounter with the F1 involved me and a prostitute sitting smoking crack together before doing the business. My second encounter was much more memorable.

Myself and my mate picked up a lady and took her back to the F1. There's something quite embarrassing about two friends being laid next to each other, as naked as the day they were born, especially when his cock was twice the size of mine! When we spit-roasted that girl there was no cheesy American high fiving, just a good old English thumbs up and a wink. I was hanging out the back of that girl with a smile on my face.

Me and that mate of mine had several memorable encounters together with the ladies of the night. There was one girl who took us back to a townhouse in the centre of Middlesbrough. When we entered the house we were frostily greeted by a pimp. This is the only time in my life that I have ever met a pimp and the reason for him being there will soon become clear.

We had to take in turns with this girl, my mate went upstairs with her first whilst I sat in the front room with this pimp. Whilst I was waiting for my sloppy seconds this pimp was pacing the room. He had a face that looked like a giant had stood on it and tucked into the back of his tracksuit bottoms was a kitchen knife! Just to make the situation a bit more uncomfortable a strange, scrawny little man wearing ridiculous pyjamas burst into the room shouting,

"What's going on?! This is a respectable B&B!"

The pimp simply looked at him and told him to fuck off. After a short argument the strange little freak did as he was told.

When my mate came back down he decided to wait for me in the street rather than in the company of that delightful man. I will never forget the smell of that bedroom when I first walked in, it was fucking disgusting. The air in the room was warm and thick and filled my lungs straight away, anyone who baulks easily couldn't have entered it.

The girl told me to lay on the bed and said she was going to do a striptease, which was a new one me. She basically just wiggled her hips and pulled my jeans off leaving them on the floor at the foot of the bed. After that she stopped wiggling, walked to the side of the bed and just took her clothes off normally. It was impossible to have enjoyable sex in that fucking disgusting room. In the end I couldn't even cum, I got dressed and left. As me and my mate were walking for a taxi he suddenly realised that £30 was missing from his pocket and then I realised a fresh box of fags was missing from my pocket! I asked him about this stupid striptease and if she'd took his jeans off, to which he replied that she had. The scam became obvious in an instant! Some scruffy cunt had been laid under the bed going through our pockets whilst we'd been doing the business! Hence the scumbag with a knife downstairs in case they were rumbled. Dear reader, how does a respectable man like myself end up in places like that?

That same lad and I were sat in a taxi once, he was in the front seat and I was sat in the back with a prossy. I was sat talking to her when all of a sudden she started having an epileptic fit! The driver immediately stopped the car, I tried my best to keep her under control and my coward mate leapt from the taxi and ran fifteen feet before stopping and looking back to see what was going on! After her fit, she sat there unconscious, by now the driver had rang for an ambulance. When she came to she was very confused, when I told her what had happened she burst into tears. I let her cuddle into me and sat with her for the full twenty minutes that it took for the ambulance to arrive. See dear reader, I am a nice man deep down. I mocked my coward friend for a long time after that.

There's slight part of me that feels a touch guilty when referring to these girls as whores. Some of them were really nice people and you couldn't help feeling sorry for them but then that wasn't always the case. Some of those girls were fucking evil and I mean pure evil, they wouldn't think twice about robbing you and if they'd watched you being stabbed in the street they wouldn't have battered an eyelid! The reason I did it so many times? It was easy sex, it always felt naughty and sometimes it felt dangerous. It was all to come to an abrupt end though.

16
NINE YEARS OF COMPLETE PEACE AND HARMONY

I have a juxtaposed personality dear reader. At work I generally dislike a lot the people I'm surrounded by but I refuse to stab them in the back and although I've been labelled a pervert I never once cheated on my wife. For those of you who don't already know Barry J Steel isn't my real name. Anyone thinking that I'm making false claims to keep my ex-wife happy, needs to know that she doesn't have a clue about my books. (Even if she did, I can't stand the cunt anymore anyway). I have a dual personality, the sober me, who I think is a gentleman and then the devil in me. This devil has finally got a name, Barry J Steel!

At the age of twenty-two I met my future wife and my life completely changed. I was a very lucky man, she was one of the good ones and she became my best mate. (A word of warning though dear reader, if you ever leave a woman, even the good ones turn into bastards!) My days of being a pervert stopped immediately, although my old friend porn was never too far away. So committed to being a one woman man was I, that I cancelled two previously made arrangements.

The first was a visit to an annual hardcore strip show that takes place in the function room of a Teesside pub, which shall remain unnamed. During this show the year before I had been laughed off the stage by the 200 strong crowd, whilst getting my little dick sucked off by one of the strippers.

The second arrangement I cancelled was a trip to Amsterdam with my mates. I had been sat with my girlfriend when one of them rang me up from the city and told me that one of the lads had received a blowjob from a ladyboy by mistake. Apparently he'd walked back out onto the street with tears in his eyes! A couple of weeks later I was sat in a pub with this lad. This conversation with him happened nine years before I was to have my own experience with ladyboy's. Everyone knew he'd had a blowjob but he hadn't told anyone the full story. I said to him,

"So you must have been angry when you found out it was really a bloke?"

He looked me in the eyes and with total seriousness came out word for word with this line,

"I was so angry…I fucking bummed it!"

I settled right down dear reader, eventually the drugs came to a complete stop and were replaced with a passion for whisky. When I got married I never ever dreamed that I would one day get divorced… but there was a moment in the immediate aftermath of my wedding when I did feel a bit depressed. Maybe depressed is too strong a word and maybe this is something that just happens to every man but I spent two or three months with a bit of regret. Regretting not doing a lot of things in my life that I could've done before I'd settled down. The main one of them all was not going to Thailand…if only I'd known back then what was to come!

I'm not going to take you through the full nine years of my relationship. All you need to know is that for seven years of it I was as happy as it's possible to be in a one woman relationship…completely frustrated and very addicted to porn! Towards the end of the relationship I was far happier fucking my hand than I was her. The collapse of my marriage wasn't caused by infidelity, it was caused by an abortion and that's all I'm going to say on the matter.

17
BLOODLUST IN ROME

About one year before my wife and I split up we had a weekend in Rome together. I can remember that even at that point I was thinking to myself, *'if this weekend turns into one big argument then it's time to call it a day'* As it turned out we got on better than what we had done in a long time and it managed to prolong our marriage a little while longer.

The first thing that struck me about Rome wasn't the magnificent architecture or the horrendous graffiti covering the city…it was the Roman people themselves. What a pack of rude, ignorant bastards they are, they're up there with the Russians! I can remember saying to my wife that I wished the English were more like them, then maybe our country wouldn't have so many problems.

We did all the tourist spots that weekend and the one I will remember the most was the Coliseum. It's an impressive place once you get over the fact that its 70% rebuild! Our tour guide walked our group around telling us the gruesome history of the place. I tried to imagine it in my mind dear reader, but I found that no matter how hard I tried, I just couldn't…because four loud Yanks wouldn't shut the fuck up! This poor tour guide was trying to do his job but he was constantly hindered by their inane and stupid questions! One particularly loud woman within their group said something that has stayed with me,

"Oh my God! You can't believe what people watched back then!"

At the time I remember thinking, *'I wish you were down there now, being hacked to pieces!'* But it was later in the day that I really thought about her words and I came to realise that I don't think people have changed at all. I can remember when the Iraqi beheading videos first came out and I was sat with a group of mates. A mobile phone was being passed around with one of these videos showing. I was the only one within the group who didn't watch it. Not because I'm some sort of fanny dear reader, but because when I was young I watched a VHS called Executions and I know from experience that once you watch something horrible then you can never unsee it. I have never even watched the Saddam Hussein execution.

So it seems to me that the majority of people still have a curiosity for the grotesque. I can remember walking down Stockton High Street one day and this particular day I just happened to take notice of all the people shuffling up and down it. They were the same people who have been shuffling up and down it since I was a kid. That high street is the centre of their miserable lives, they get out of bed on a morning, have their breakfast and then head straight for the high street where they can start their day of shuffling. (The song Bittersweet Symphony by the Verve always reminds me of these people) A thought crossed my mind…if Stockton Borough Council one day announced that there was to be a public hanging in the high-street, in what direction do you think these people would start to shuffle dear reader? I can guarantee that it wouldn't be away from the execution, in fact I'd place a bet that Stockton High Street would be overflowing that day!

Now let's imagine that all of England's most notorious child killers were rounded up. It was decided that they were going to be fed to a pack of starved lion's right in the middle of Wembley Stadium. Tickets were to cost £10 each and the best seats were to sell for £20 each. Dear reader, even Pink Floyd themselves couldn't sell as many tickets as what that show would. This is universal by the way, there isn't a stadium in the entire world that wouldn't be filled by crowds baying for the blood of criminals in this modern age! That thick Yank came out with the stupidest statement known to man…because man hasn't changed one little bit. I wish I'd thought of all this the very moment she came out with it, I would've given her it both barrels!

18
I HATE EVERYTHING!
PART TWO

MULTICULTURALISM- After the Second World War black people were brought to England from Jamaica to fill the jobs lost by men who died fighting for their country. These immigrants came over and they dressed and talked like the indigenous people of their new home nation. Although there is racism in England and always will be, the integration of the black community has largely been a successful one.

It may surprise people to learn that it was actually a Tory who suggested bringing multiculturalism to the UK. This bloke decided that the phrase *'when in Rome do as the Romans'* was old hat. He suggested that all immigrants coming to Britain from now on should bring their own culture with them and carry on living as they had in their home country. He must have been out of his fucking mind!

Cut to modern day Britain, an extremely overcrowded island that has double the population of that huge country Canada! Up and down this tiny little island are segregated communities, living side by side with absolute hatred for one another. Most of this hatred is within the immigrant communities themselves. They've been herded together with other religions they hate and people from countries that they despise. It's a ticking time bomb, caused by one stupid do-gooder who must have really hated his country.

England today... grown men marry little girls in secret, torsos of children murdered in voodoo rituals are found in the capital, people protest against not being able to set fire to their dead loved ones and then sail them down the Tyne, women walk the streets in death shrouds, men murder their own daughters because they refuse to marry their cousins, white people are beaten to within an inch of their lives for walking down the wrong street, retired indigenous people are forced to sell their houses to pay for their own care that yesterday's immigrant gets for free and English soldiers are hacked to pieces in the street by Muslims for wearing the wrong t-shirt!

Yes Britain truly is great! Let's all agree now that multiculturalism DOESN'T mean segregation, animosity and religious violence. No not at all, let's all agree that multiculturalism means lasting peace and harmony. BULLSHIT!

Human beings are a species of animal...if an animal moves to a new habitat it has to learn to adapt to its new environment, the environment doesn't adapt for the animal! If you want to live in someone else's country firstly leave your stupid, backwards religion at the door, learn the language, embrace the culture and fucking dress properly.

WHEN IN ROME DO AS THE ROMANS!

PEOPLE WHO CRY OVER DEAD CELEBRITIES- This chapter was going to be called '*people who cry over people they've never met'*. When I sat and thought about it that wouldn't be fair, every now and again there's a news story that is so horrendous, it's bound to have women in tears. People who cry over celebrities on the other hand are wankers and they really piss me off. (A bloke at work actually admitted to me that he criedwhen the actor who played Father Ted died…do you remember that Paul?)

Unless you personally know someone then you are never going know what a person is really like. Even saint Mother Teresa had a very chequered past if you care to research into it! Celebrities court the media and they use the media to portray a false image of themselves which the public will like. People who become celebrities are always insecure people who really crave attention. When they don't get attention they pull hissy fits and go into states of depression. '*Poor me* another one!'

What is worse than these emotionally insecure attention seekers? The people who feel sorry for them without even knowing them! When Princess Diana and Michael Jackson died, thousands of people were in floods of tears. None of them actually knew these people, how many of these thousands have been to funerals of people they actually knew and didn't cry? I'll bet it's a lot.

I'm tempted to slag off Princess Diana but at the end of the day she's somebody's mother, so I'm not going to. Michael Jackson on the other hand didn't have any kids so I can say what I like about him. (Anyone who believes that those dazzling white kids are his must be really, really, really thick!). The people who cried over Michael Jackson must all have something wrong with their brains. We all know what he was! I would like to meet some of these people and I would ask them one simple question,

'If one of your neighbours looked and talked like Michael Jackson and he knocked on your door, telling you he had a big playground in his back garden and could your kids spend the night at his. What would you say to him?'

I'm pretty sure I know what the answer would be but when fame and money become involved people seem to lose their senses. There is something that I wish everyone would realise, after gypo's and dole scum, entertainers are the least important people in society. If you find that you look up to somebody just because that person has been on Big Brother then you must be fucking mentally deranged!

Dear reader, no one truly knows anyone, don't cry for strangers, it's a waste of good tears.

DO-GOODERS- Ultra right-wing people destroy groups of people's lives, ultra left-wing people destroy countries! Do-gooders live their entire lives with blinkers on, they won't listen to facts and they won't listen to anybody else's opinion. Do-gooders have completely fucked my country and they won't even admit it, in fact they'd be happy to make it even worse. Worker's rights in England have gotten a lot worse instead of getting a lot better. Companies have managed to do this with the direct help of do-gooders. The spineless foreign employees in this country now, who only care about money and not about their own safety or rights has fucked it up for the natives.

If a do-gooder was to read this book they would label me a bigot and a racist but I'm not. Aside from a couple of harmless racist jokes, all I've done is tell the truth. Do-gooders don't listen to the truth, they only care about their own nonsensical ideology. I've already said that the most racist people in England today are the immigrants themselves, only a week before writing this chapter a Pakistani taxi driver was moaning to me about Eastern Europeans!

The fact is, these do-gooders can't claim to be completely racist free anyway. Its human nature. Imagine a white, Christian do-gooder couple, their daughter turns up at their door with her new boyfriend. When they open the door they are confronted by a dark skinned man with a long beard and he's dressed in sheets. What's going to be the first thing that crosses their minds? Reverse the situation, what's going to go through the Muslim parents minds when they see their son with a white girl in a short skirt?

Do-gooders just don't live in the real world. They think everything works out perfect and they refuse to accept things when they don't. They need to stop pretending that they're saints and they need to apologise to the rest of us for doing the irreparable damage that they've done to our country!

CIRCUMCISION- There's two types of circumcision in this fucked up modern world, the religious type and the fashion type. I hate both. (Medical circumcision is not included in this chapter)

Religious circumcision is proof enough that religion makes people behave in a depraved, backwards way. Imagine the birth of your son, the nurse hands the new born baby to you and rather than your first thought being, 'What a beautiful baby' its 'We'll have to get the end of that cock chopped off!' Which mental case decided that a natural part of the human body should be removed in the name of God? It actually stems from organised religions fear and distaste of sex. You didn't see the Pagans shy away from nudity or shagging, they were at it like rabbits. Then Judaism came along and from Judaism spawned two more equally grotesque religion's Christianity and Islam. All three with a morbid fear of sex. The simple fact is male circumcision desensitises the bellend (glans for the educated idiots), making sex less pleasurable. Female circumcision normally removes the full labia, destroying the girl's future sex life. In England female circumcision is illegal but male isn't, I wonder why that is? Apart from it being barbaric and backwards, circumcision is morally wrong. How can a person's own decisions about what happens to their own body be taken away from them?

Even worse than religious circumcision is what has been happening in America for the last decade. Young American men purposely have their foreskins cut off because it's fashionable! They've been watching these 'cut cocks' on porno's and decided '*it looks a bit better*'. How thick can people be?! It's only after they get it done and realise that their exposed bellend is uncomfortably chaffing against their boxer shorts that they realise what the foreskin was for. They only have to put up with the constant irritation for about six months though, after that time they've lost all the sensitivity in the bellend that used to make a blowjob feel so good.

I hate people acting like sheep dear reader, but when it comes to something as stupid this it makes the mind boggle. We are lucky in England right now, circumcised kids still get bullied at school but the change is coming. They say we are always ten years behind America, what happens there will eventually happen here. This 'fashionable circumcision' is just around the corner for our youth. I've already got my plan in place for when my son grows up and suggests it. I'm going to tell him to tape his foreskin back for 24 hours and make his mind up then.

ONLY CHILDREN- I know two grown men who are both only children. These men have never met each other before but their similarities are uncanny. They are both mingebag's, they both hate women but they constantly need a girlfriend, both are divorced, both have strained relationships with their kids, both love knowing everybody else's business but hate people knowing theirs and both are absolute mammy's boys.

We all know that only kids are fucking weird. When I was a kid one of my friends was an only child, his parents didn't let him play away from the street until he was 12! He had countryside at the bottom of his road but he wasn't allowed to go and play in it! How could his parents expect him to be normal if they didn't let him do normal things? (He grew up to be a fuck up by the way) All only children's weirdness stems directly from their parents. They generally have two problems in childhood.

Firstly they are always spoilt rotten and sharing things is something that they are never taught and never learn. These are the kids in school who refuse to lend out their pens! As adults I would imagine it's hard to live with these people because of their inability to share.

Their second problem is the biggest one of all. It's called *'overbearing mother syndrome'*. These men will be mammy's boys for their entire life. These overbearing mothers will tell their son's their opinion on absolutely everything! Saying things to them that no mother should ever say. No matter how nice their girlfriends are, they will never be good enough in mammy's eyes.

Only children, you are all mental fuck ups…but it's not your fault.

ZERO-HOUR CONTRACTS- One simple fact about life in Britain, worker's rights have gotten worse instead of better. Our rights peaked in the seventies and they've been gradually getting worse ever since. When workers were at the top of their powers they did what is only human nature…they completely ruined it for themselves! The unions had become so powerful that they could hold the government to ransom.

In my life as a contractor I've heard many stories of what workers could get away with in the seventies. I'll always remember one chap telling me that he and his work colleagues had turned up for work one day. Apparently the weather was absolutely beautiful this day and the lads decided they would rather be at home or sat outside a pub. Together they gathered all the toilet roll on site and threw it in a skip, they then sent the steward into the management's office to tell them that there was no bog roll so they were walking off site! Now gentlemen this was never going to last forever and it didn't.

Maggie Thatcher was a heartless bitch, she was nearly as heartless as that cunt Tony Blair, but not quite in the same league. When she moved into number 10 she had no choice but to strip the unions of some of their powers. The problem was she stripped too many and they carry on being stripped today and our unions have gotten weaker and more corrupt.

In modern day Britain, zero-hour contracts have gone from something only found in pizza shops to rapidly becoming the norm. How this slap in the face to workers has happened is beyond me. I've got a terrible feeling that in ten years' time I'll be on one myself. What's the point in any of us being in unions if companies are allowed to get away with this? I'm assuming you already know what a zero-hour contract is, if you don't know then it basically means a company can turn round one week and tell you to work 60 hours and then the next week they can say they have nothing for you. There's no statutory holiday pay and you aren't allowed to work for anyone else because you have to be on call!

If I was ever put on one then I know I would use it in my favour, Monday mornings would become a thing of the past, I don't really like Wednesdays either. I hope every contractor will have these same ideas in mind, although no doubt the wretches would spoil it for everyone as usual. If they try to do it to us and the unions aren't interested then let's all use it against the companies until they have to scrap the fucking things.

NOISY DEFECATORS- I can remember when I was in my early twenties I had a spell working in a horrible fab-shop. To anyone who's never worked in one of these, all you need to know is that they are modern day workhouses. At the time I was working with my best mate and every day we would take in turns to have a half hour skive in the toilets. Although this probably sounds weird and possibly a little bit perverse to some people, believe me, the shithouses are the only places you can hide in those types of hellholes!

So each day we'd take in turns, watching each other's backs and swapping newspapers. One day I had just had my spell and then my mate went for his, he returned after only ten minutes.

"Why are you back so early?"

"I had to get out, it was fucking horrible!"

It transpired that the moment he locked himself in the cubicle a man went into the cubicle next door to him. The man instantly began shitting and whilst doing so he was grunting. My mate went onto to explain that after two minutes of this the cubicle on the other side of him also became occupied. Again some bloke had come for a shite and after a loud fart this man also started grunting whilst he was filling the pot. So my mate is sat there in the middle trying to read a newspaper and on either side of him are noisy, smelly, grunting men. I almost felt sorry for my friend.

Now I've been having poo's all my life dear reader and although I don't profess to being an expert in the art of defecating, I do know that there is absolutely no need to sit there grunting! If you are one of these grunters then please, next time you're having a poo just pause for a moment and ask yourself, *'do I really need to be making these noises?'*

PART THREE

THE TENS

19
THE OFFSHORE WILDERNESS

The single best decision that I have ever made in my life was my decision to go and work offshore in the North Sea. I actually completed my survival training course the week after my wife and I split up! This was pure coincidence, the course had been booked a month in advance but it couldn't have come at a better time. You will hear men say that an oilrig is no place to have personal problems, which may be correct if you are in a relationship but when you're single then the opposite is true. I found that being out in the middle of the North Sea was a welcome break from any problems I may have been having at the time. Offshore is where you can forget about the real world for a couple of weeks. Overnight a job that I had always hated suddenly made me feel extremely lucky to have it.

Before I actually worked offshore I used to imagine oilrigs to be futuristic type places with all the top of the range tools. Its only when you get on them that you realise that they're nothing more than big rusty skips with absolutely fuck all gear on them!

I have the heart of a poet dear reader, and when I went out onto the rig on my very first day I was struck by the beauty of the surrounding scenery. An endless sight of waves, with boats and other rigs on the horizon, clouds in all sorts of formations… The North Sea sunsets are the best sunsets that I have ever seen in my life, better than Ibiza and better than Thailand (although the surroundings in the two places are slightly better). I have been told that the sight of all that sea sends some men stir crazy and some people have only lasted a day or two before demanding to be flown back to land. I don't know what the idiots were expecting!

So why do men choose to work on an oilrig? The time off work, it's as simple as that. 'Normal' people may struggle to get their heads around why we do it but us offshore workers struggle to get our heads around why people wouldn't. Who wants to get out of bed every morning in the darkness, scrape the ice of your car windows and then join the morning commute to the place you hate? Working at least five days out of seven and spending a few hours with your family each night? It's a dog's life! I've been offshore over two years at the time of writing this and I've never had so much time off! As it stands I keep having one month long holidays in Thailand with about three or four months separating each holiday! Who wouldn't want that?! If the price I have to pay is living on an oilrig a little bit of the year then so be it. By the way don't think my time is 50/50 between offshore and home because it isn't, it's not even close.

In 2014 I worked a total of 14 weeks offshore! (Admittedly I had a little spell of unemployment at the end of the year and also I don't expect to be this lucky every year!) It's a brilliant life but you just have to be willing to take the rough with the smooth.

When you work offshore you find out just how strange people are. It's not like onshore where people you don't like are easily avoided. You have to live with your work mates and some of them can be very trying. Forget about work wretches, I've moaned enough about them already and trust me there's plenty offshore, but it's on a rig where everyone is exposed to each other's little routines and eccentricities.

I heard a story about one man with two eccentricities. Apparently this man was always completely naked in his bedroom regardless of whether he was sharing with someone else and also he wouldn't use the ladder when climbing into his top bunk, he would pull off some hop, skip, jump manoeuvre! One night his roommate was laid in the bottom bunk watching the telly when this weird bloke climbed down from the top bunk to go and use the toilet, bollock naked. When he had finished he came back into the room and he pulled off his jumping into the top bunk trick, as he did it the poor bloke laid on the bottom bunk was hit it the cheek by a stray drop of piss! (If the naked man should ever read this book I want you to know that I think you sound like an absolute dickhead!)

Depending on the rig you may have to share a bedroom with a complete stranger. You shake hands, have some small talk and then quickly work out a routine between you both. Every man needs personal time for a shower and a wank. You then spend the first night wondering if your new roommate is a snorer, it can be a tense wait. I once had to share a room with a man who seemed very nice but his snoring was like nothing I had ever heard before in my life…even with earplugs in and a pillow over my head! After the first night I asked for a room change but it was unavailable, I lasted two more nights and on the fourth morning feeling very tired and very pissed off I asked for a room change again. Luckily I got it this time, if I hadn't I was going to demand to be flown off the rig. His snoring was that bad that losing the job wouldn't have bothered me!

The worst roommate I've had so far was a young lad who suffered from night terrors! He was actually a really nice lad and he didn't work offshore fulltime, he was only on for four nights to do some specialist job. He would always fall asleep before me and I would have to listen to him swearing and fighting in his sleep. On one of the nights though I was woken up at around 02:00 by loud blood curdling screams! When I say screams, I mean SCREAMS! It was at the top of his lungs and I absolutely shit myself! Nothing was mentioned between us the next day.

I'm going to give a special mention to the rope-access lads here because there's fucking loads of them offshore! They are affectionately nicknamed the 'dopes on ropes', I prefer to call them the 'yes men'. This breed of men all seem to have a similar background. They left school and then decided that they wanted to travel the world to try and *'find themselves'*. They eventually get home and realise that they don't have any qualifications so they start to complete as many semi-skilled courses as they can. Eventually they end up in my industry, it's completely alien to them, they've never heard of Health & Safety and they don't know what unions are, all they know is that they're finally earning decent money. They will do any job thrown at them without question, I've seen these blokes do things a black man working in a diamond mine would refuse to do! They're all fucking idiots the lot of them!

I can remember after my very first trip offshore when the helicopter landed. I got off it in my one piece survival suit and I felt like an astronaut returning from the moon. Like anything you soon get used to it though. It's a brilliant feeling when your feet finally hit terra firma and you know you are only ten minutes away from being in the Spiders Web and having your first pint of lager in two weeks. All your time off laid out in front of you. Some people live abroad, lots of men fly straight down to Spain. You might be going on holiday (which you could do every month if you wanted to) or have some DIY planned, maybe you just want to lay on a settee and get pissed. It doesn't matter, it's entirely up to you and no one can do anything to change it. If there's any justice in the world then I will never have to work onshore again, because that truly is the mugs life.

20
FAT LADIES LOVE A GOOD FISTING

About two months after I left my wife I went out one night and got completely fucking smashed. I can't really remember the night at all but what I do remember is the end of it. My memory starts with me being stood on a street outside a club and I'm kissing a fat bird. I have no doubt that this woman has completely taken advantage of me in my drunken state. She was fat but she was tanned and had a pretty face.

I can remember this woman pulling me into a taxi and then next thing we're in the front room of the flat I was renting at the time. This creature was sucking my face off as we laid on my settee, there was a bit of boob fondling and groping. The next thing I remember is her being knelt on my carpet with her belly on my settee. Dear reader, I honestly can't remember how she got into this position but I took advantage of it. Her dress was lifted up and her big knickers were pulled down. I stuck two fingers straight in and they barely touched the sides. Three fingers went in as easily as the two, then my knuckles went in as easily as the fourth finger had and my thumb knuckle was no problem at all. By now I'd seen enough fisting porn to pick up on the technique, my mistakes of my youth were well and truly behind me. From two fingers in to being wrist deep can't have taken any longer than a minute. There was no lube involved, just her giant sweaty fanny and my dry hand! It was a strange sight, seeing my hand completely disappear but I have to admit, it was also a very good one.

Can you remember when you were young and loved watching anal porn? When you watched it, it looked marvellous and you couldn't wait until the day that you could do it yourself. When you did finally meet a girl mucky enough to try it you couldn't help feeling slightly disappointed. Turns out it looks better than what it actually is. (Just like Ibiza)

Dear reader, I can assure you now that when you fist a girl there is no such feeling of disappointment whatsoever. It's absolutely fucking brilliant! That girl was on her knees in the front room of my flat with my fist and half my wrist up her and she was screaming! I've never had a squirter in my life and this girl wasn't one either but she was dripping all over my carpet.

After her final scream I retrieved my soggy hand and attempted to mount her. There was no way I was even going to attempt to put it in her gaping wizards sleeve so I went straight for the bullethole instead. The problem was I was absolutely wrecked, my semi on didn't have the strength to penetrate, it kept bending on impact. I gave up and went to bed. When I woke up the next morning she was gone. Treasured memories.

21
PROSTITUTES PART THREE
A NEW BEGINNING

I know that I handled my divorce very well dear reader but when I look back now at the first six months of being single, you could say that I went off the rails a teeny bit. After nine years of practically being celibate, a beast was unleashed onto the world. At first I was happy going out every weekend and having one night stands. Then the arguments over my kids with the ex started and I hit a new phase. It was my woman hating phase. After these arguments started, I suddenly found that I had absolutely no interest in anything a woman had to say anymore. This made getting tapped up a little bit difficult. Cue my return to the world of prostitution. (I memorably bummed one in somebody's back garden!)

After a couple of months of shagging Teesside's finest crackwhores I had woken one morning up to find my mobile phone had been stolen by the lovely lady whose company I had paid for the night before. The last thing I remember was her giving me a blowjob, I must have passed out during it. She kindly robbed me of my mobile phone and left me sleeping, if the thick bitch had bothered to look she would have seen £1000 in Thai baht in my top drawer. When I realised what had happened I sat there feeling like shit and asked myself what the fuck I was doing. I was a father now, my days of romancing crack scum should be well behind me. Shortly after that episode I was off to Thailand for what would become a life changing holiday.

A website was recommended to me by a work colleague. Type the words ADULT and WORK into google and you can't go wrong. This site tells you all about escorts in your area. You can see photos of them, see their prices, what they're up for, fucking allsorts. It's a perverts dream and it put an end to my flirting's with crackwhores. You just sit in your front room and wait for them to arrive, they do their business and then fuck off. It's magic. You'd be surprised at just how many lasses are on that site and some of them look like models!

One night I ordered a girl off the website and I told her she would have to run me up to a cash machine. She said OK and when she got to my house I came out and jumped into her car. She wasn't driving dear reader, her boyfriend was in the driver's seat! After she introduced him to me I broke the ice by saying,

"Well this is a bit fucking weird isn't it?!"

We got chatting and before too long the dirty bastard asked if I wanted him to join in! There are some right fucking perverts in this world dear reader!

The lass must have sensed my unease because she explained that a lot of men liked that sort of thing. It wasn't for me, I got him to run me to the bank and then I fucked his girlfriend in my bedroom whilst he sat outside waiting.

Now that my woman hating phase has passed, my prostitute shenanigans have mainly fizzled out. It's basically all just in Thailand now, but you'd have to read my first book if you want to hear about them.

22
MY THEORY ABOUT BINGE DRINKING

We British are a nation of big drinkers and these days we are bombarded by adverts telling us the dangers of excessive drinking. Our alcoholic politicians have bogus think tanks trying to come up with ideas on how to stop us all. All they ever come up with is raising taxes, '*Put an end to cheap alcohol!*' they scream. Anyone who's been to Spain knows that we don't have cheap alcohol in this country. I have my own theory of why we drink so much and if I'm correct it means we are NEVER going to change. I promise that I haven't stolen this theory, if anyone else has come up with it then we must just have similar, and might I add genius, minds.

Britain is a draconian nation, it always has been and it always will be. In recent years we have tried to veer towards a more 'gently, gently' American management style but that old bully boss attitude is still there. From Monday to Friday adults are treated like little children at work, they are talked down to and bullied. When they leave work it doesn't end there, people can't go anywhere without seeing signs telling them what to do and what not to do.

In my own place of work the toilets have signs telling me to flush the chain and another sign telling me to wash my hands! We are bullied in our cars, bullied in our shopping centres, there's fucking cameras EVERYWHERE watching our every move! Every single adult is treated like a child and a criminal.

If you think England is draconian try going to Scotland, it's even worse! They have more cameras, more signs, it can be hard to breathe! In my job I have to go to a heliport every month, inside the heliport I have my bag searched, my body padded down, newspapers are searched and even my passport has been flicked through! Some of the jobsworth's get right up close to you to see if they can smell alcohol on your breath! I'm being treated like a criminal and all I'm trying to do is get to fucking work! None of this happened when I worked in Europe by the way.

On the subject of being in Europe, the rig I was on had a hardcore porn channel on the TV. No porn sites were blocked on the internet either. Now I haven't worked on every British rig but all the ones I've worked on so far have internet porn blocked! Every man on the planet watches porn, were does this stupid British prudishness come from? Thousands of men stuck on rig's in the middle of the sea and we aren't allowed porn! Do they expect us all to turn 'prison gay' for a fortnight! It's just another example of draconianism.

We have a government who censors this and bans that, telling us what we're allowed to watch and what we can put in our bodies. I'll bet the Dutch don't feel like children. The do-gooders trying to stop us from drinking and smoking never ask the question, '*Why do we do it*?' They just want it banned along with all the other fun things! (Can I just take this opportunity to say Mary Whitehouse was a cunt! Good riddance! People like her shouldn't be allowed to exist!)

So this is our lives, spend five days out of seven in a place we hate, being talked to like children. What do they expect people to do with their shitty two days off? They are going to get absolutely smashed so they can forget about the five days of hell they've just been put through. Can't the government and health scientists see this simple fact? Are they all really so blind to it? If they want the drinking to stop they need to tear down the signs, smash all the cameras, cut working hours, raise wages and sack all the bullies!

But no. It's easier just to make drink more expensive. It won't solve the problem but at least they'll get even more revenue from the already overtaxed children. I say fuck it, let's carry on binge drinking because there's absolutely fuck all else for us to do!

23
TEACHERS ARE DIRTY

Over the course of my working life I've met quite a few men who have told me the same thing…teachers are filthy in the bedroom! Part of me has wished this isn't true because my mother is a teacher. But in 2013 I was to discover for myself that teachers are very, very dirty. Well some of them…please mam, say it's only some of them.

The woman I'm referring to I met three times altogether. After the third time I didn't really want to see her again, it was a bit too much for me. She was 37 at the time and a secondary school teacher. The first two times I was with her nothing out of the ordinary happened but then the last time she turned into some sort of crazed sex fiend! She came to my house and hit the vodka straight away, by the time we got to the bedroom we were both smashed. When I think back to this little episode now I'm pretty sure she had the same mind-set as the girl from chapter 14. I think she had secret fantasies about being raped!

We were kissing on my bed, then the titty sucking started, when I went to put my hand down her knickers she suddenly started saying, "No, no!" But she wasn't saying it her own voice, she was putting on a childlike voice. I thought it was a bit queer but I just let her get on with it, I took off her jeans and knickers and then tried to open her legs. She locked them tight and started babbling the same shit again!

"What're you doing?!" I asked her.

She stopped babbling and stared at me, looking at me as if to say '*what's wrong*?' She relaxed her legs and I took the opportunity to go down on her. The babbling started immediately but by now I'd sussed out that it was just some weird fetish of hers. I was getting on with it when suddenly she locked my head between her thighs, squeezing it really fucking tight! Next thing I know I'm involved in a wrestling match and we actually rolled off the bed onto the floor. Dear reader, all I wanted to do was have a shag and go to sleep but it became clear that this psychopath was wanting to make me fight for sex and overpower her.

When we were back on the bed there was a point where she was on her knees with her arse in the air, I had three fingers in her biff and her head pinned down with my knee. I can tell you now that I was pushing down with some amount of force, if it had been my own head pinned down like that I think I would've started crying. I spanked her, fucked in her in the minge, fucked her up the arse and skull fucked her till she choked. Some parts I enjoyed and some of it just wasn't for me. When I was having to fight and wrestle

I really, really couldn't be bothered with it. When my tiddle was inside of something then I was happy.

The next morning I was laid on my settee and she was laid on top of me cuddling into my chest. I can remember looking down at her and thinking, '*I just want you out of my house*.' When she finally did decide to leave she went to kiss me, I turned my face and give her my cheek. It was a simple gesture to let her know I never wanted to see the crazy bitch ever again. When you meet a girl like that you can't help but wonder to yourself, '*What the fuck happened to you in your childhood?*'

24
THE ORIGIN OF FAECES

I've shat myself twice in my life…I got away with it both times.

25
GOODBYE SMELLY BELLEND!

Dear reader, do you suffer from a smelly bellend? If the answer is yes then consider me your knight in shining armour. I've had a completely odour free penis for over a year now. My knob didn't actually stink, but no matter how many scrubs and washes it was never completely odour free. It was something I was never really arsed about until after my divorce. When you find yourself suddenly single in your thirties you start to worry about things that have never bothered you before.

I went to a doctors and had a mole removed from my neck, my average weight dropped by a stone and then there was this smelly bellend business. In January 2013 I had my first holiday in Thailand, by the time I came home I had a complex. Those Thai girls seem to have an acute sense of smell. When their noses twitched around my bellend it was quite embarrassing. I decided to do some research to find a cure.

I found a thread on the internet that had been started by some complaining woman. She was moaning about the stench of her new boyfriends cock and banging on about how perfectly fresh smelling her ex-boyfriends tail had been. Like me, she wanted to find a cure. Some brave man had replied to her question and he revealed a secret known only to a golden few.

Dear reader, I reveal to you now that treasured secret. Hydrogen Peroxide. A natural mix of air and water that kills bacteria on impact. It's available over the counter in pharmacies and costs £1 a bottle. You need to buy the type that's labelled 'For use as mouthwash' (NOT the food grade stuff!), it comes in three different percentages 3%, 6% or 9%. You can use any of these. Some of the pharmacy jobsworth's might ask you what you're going to use it for, just tell them mouthwash. If you have no shame then feel free to proudly and loudly say,

"I'm going to wash my smelly cock with it!"

When you get it home pour some onto a cotton wool bud and give your smelly bellend a good rub down. It will smell like roses for the next three days.

I said in the introduction that if it's possible I would like to educate you a tiny bit. If you haven't learned anything in this book so far then I believe that has just changed.

**Any penal damage caused by rubbing hydrogen peroxide onto ones member is wholly the responsibility of the member's owner. Dr Barry J Steel cannot be held accountable.*

26
RAPED BY A DEMON

When I first started seeing my ex-wife it took a couple of months before I was allowed to sleep at her parents' house. The first night I slept there she told me that the house was haunted by a pervert ghost. Her reason for believing this was because one night she had woken up and was being pinned down to the bed by an invisible force. She said she was wide awake at the time and laid on her back, she could feel a pair of hands pushing down on her tits and she was completely unable to move. This ordeal lasted for around one minute and when the force vanished she sat up absolutely terrified.

Dear reader, I don't believe in ghosts or any other such nonsense. If you believe in ghosts then I'm telling you now that you're wrong. If you've had a supernatural experience in your life I can assure you it was your mind playing tricks on you. Our brains are extremely powerful and strange things. Just recently I was sat on a train listening to my iPod. A song came on that reminded me of watching Glastonbury on the telly, at that point I got a shiver down my spine and my arms became covered in goosebumps. This has happened to all of us many times in our lives. I don't mean music on the train, I mean the goosebumps. When it does happen we don't give it a second thought. Because I was sat on a train and bored I did give it thought. I had just had a quick flash of a memory and it had caused my skin to react. I thought to myself, '*That's a bit fucking weird really.*' Although this has absolutely nothing to do with ghosts it's just a point to prove how powerful your brain and mind are.

One of my mates works in a hospital and I was telling him the story my ex-wife had told me about the pervert ghost. He informed me that it wasn't a ghost and it's called Sleep Paralysis, apparently it's quite a common thing. Whilst in deep sleep our bodies are paralysed, some people become semiconscious in this state and when they do it feels like they are being pinned down to the bed. I told her this fact but she shrugged it off and chose to carry on believing it was a ghost. This is the typical attitude of the human species, they choose to believe in the fantastical rather than the plain old boring truth.

In April 2014 I returned home from my third trip to Thailand. I had been home two days and I was feeling miserable but just to make me feel even more miserable I had woken up to find that half my bottom lip and chin had bizarrely swollen up for some reason. I looked like a distant cousin of John Merrick. I did what any grown man would do…I rang my mam. She told me to go to a pharmacy and buy some antihistamines. (Stick with this story reader, it has got a point)

I had a very embarrassing trip to the pharmacy, trying to cover my face by pretending to scratch my lip. I got back home and read the instructions, it said I was to take one tablet a day for seven days. I took two straight away and then took another two just before bed. Due to my disgust with my appearance I thought a little overdose might help speed things up. Later on I was to wake up in the middle of the night. I sleep on my belly and when I woke up I could feel two hands pushing down on the back of my head. I could feel these hands so clearly that I could actually feel a thumb pushing into the upper part of my neck! At the time I felt wide awake and just before blind panic set in I remembered what had happened to my ex and what my mate had told me. Once I realised what was happening I remained calm and waited for this strange experience to end. Just like with my ex it seemed to last for around one minute. This bit is hard to explain but after it ended I woke up properly. Although I felt wide awake at the time and I can remember it vividly, I realised I hadn't been fully awake after all. You would have to experience it for yourself to fully grasp what I'm saying.

The next day I looked up Sleep Paralysis on Wikipedia to try and find a cause for it. There was a list of reasons and theories as to why it might happen.

One explanation was an overuse of stimulants which I'm guessing is what the antihistamines must have been.

Dear reader, I can promise you now that if I hadn't known what was going on I would have absolutely shit myself and I would have spent the rest of that night believing in ghosts. If this has happened to you in the past, now you know what was going on. If this happens to you in the future then don't panic, keep calm and just remember it's your brain doing something weird. It doesn't last long.

27
MY FEAR FOR MANKIND

Not too long I was sat in my mate's front room and we were having a drink whilst we waited for his wife to get ready upstairs. We were sat talking and all the while a hair dryer was making noise. At one point I needed a piss so I went to use the toilet upstairs, when I got to the top of the stairs I received a shock. It wasn't my mate's wife using the hair dryer, it was his 18 year old step son. He was stood on the landing half naked looking in the full length mirror. On the floor next to him was a set of hair straighteners on charge! I had no option but to chastise him!

When I look at the young men of today they all look exactly the same to me. They're all muscular from using steroids, their arms are tattooed from top to bottom and they all have a fake tan and stupid trendy haircuts! (I'll bet you don't believe I'm only 33 at the time of writing this do you?) Everything today is about image, vanity in young men hasn't peaked, it's only going to get worse and worse!

Apparently when aftershave first came out the men who wore it would be bullied and ridiculed by all the 'normal' blokes. They were called poofter's and nancy boys who liked to wear perfume. I wonder what those blokes would think of today's generation of men, I'll bet they'd be spinning in their graves.

They say whatever the rich do and have, the working classes will eventually get further down the line. Plastic surgery is now available to the masses and apparently more and more men are having it. For years it's been normal for male Hollywood A-lister's to walk around wearing makeup. Today a lot of gay men have started to wear it and normal men are edging ever closer to it.

Recently on holiday in Thailand, I was waiting for my mate to get ready and he turned and asked me if I wanted to use his 'face cream'. Out of curiosity I looked at the label, dear reader that cream was a midge's dick away from being foundation! My mate tried to protest against this fact.

I have absolutely no doubt that when my young son grows up it will be normal for men to walk around wearing foundation. When he gets even older it will be normal for all men to have a facelift. It really does scare me to think of what the next generation of young men are going to look like, the ones we have now are embarrassing enough!

How am I going to look my son in the eyes and have a normal conversation with him, when he's sat there caked in makeup with a ridiculous haircut that he's just spent two hours doing? If anyone thinks I'm being farfetched trust me I'm not, this is a definite.

Unfortunately the future is going to prove all my predictions correct.

Just look at the men from the 1940's and compare them to what we have now. It's a complete disgrace what has happened to us! Spending fucking hours in clothes shops like women do, asking their mates how they look, like women do. It's fucking pathetic. It takes me 15 minutes to get ready and that's if I'm not rushing.

The next generation of men won't want to do any manual labour in case they damage the soft skin on their hands! The telly will be full of adverts with feminine products for men to buy, foundation, smooth razorblades for armpits, tampax! Even now we have adverts for men that we didn't have 15 years ago, fucking male moisturiser! Men, moisturiser doesn't do anything! We have been laughing at women for wasting money on it for years and now we are fucking doing it ourselves. If you're morbidly obsessed with having smooth skin then stop drinking, stop smoking and never go out in the sun! Rubbing expensive cream into your skin does absolutely fuck all! If you don't believe me then google it, anti-aging cream doesn't exist!

I can't actually believe that I'm sat here now writing about how men have turned into women. Just when the fuck did this happen? How the fuck did this happen? Who do we have to blame? Only ourselves and the sheep that we all are. Some dickhead watches an advert on the telly or some celebrity, he doesn't have his own mind so he goes out and does as he's been told. His thick mate sees him and decides to copy him, then his even thicker mate decides to copy that other thick mate and so on and so on…until you end up with a generation of androgynous looking men.

No cunt lives in reality anymore!

28
ISLAM RAMADANA DING DONG

I was going to slip this chapter into one of my 'I Hate Everything' chapters but then I thought, *'no, those Muslims are so special they deserve their very own chapter!'*

I don't believe in religious freedom dear reader, because different religions don't mix well, they cause segregation. In my own perfect world we would all be secular but that's never going to happen. It's therefore my belief that if people really feel the need to be deluded then a country should pick one religion and stick to it. In England you should either be Atheist or Christian but nothing else!

Before I begin my attack on Muslims I want to say that not all of them are bad and to say otherwise would be small mindedness. Like I've said earlier I don't judge anyone by their race. The colour of somebodies skin does not determine whether they are a nice person or not, but Muslims are not a race, they are followers of a religion. The first wave of Muslims who came to England were generally nice people looking for a better life. Here's the problem though, they came here because Muslim countries are fucking horrible places that they wanted to escape from, but they didn't embrace our culture, instead they kept the one that they had ran away from. Muslims do not integrate with any other community and this original segregation is what has led to all the problems that we have with Muslims in modern day England.

I've said that people need to stop caring so much about offending each other, you can't make everybody happy so what's the point in even beginning to try? There is one group of people in this modern world that everybody seems determined to not offend, that's the Muslims. Now the hysterical desire to not offend these people isn't born out of respect, it's born out of fear. Say one bad thing about Islam and you risk being murdered.

When those Danish cartoons came out a few years back, herds of backward fucking Muslims caused chaos all over the world. Here's a little known fact dear reader, the original cartoons were very tame and just a *JOKE!* In the Muslim countries a much more offensive version of the cartoons were shown to the natives. These offensive versions of the cartoons were created by Imams to cause outrage and incite hatred amongst the Muslims. That's right dear reader, it was Muslims of the highest order themselves who created those images which insulted their god!

Religions shouldn't be mixed but Islam is THE main religion that should be contained within its native countries. This breed of people are *so* different from the rest of us. What it boils down to is the fact that they haven't evolved like the rest of us, they live with a Stone Age mentality. (To any *head in the sand* do-gooder reading this then I'd like to ask you one question…name me a Muslim country you would like to emigrate to?) When they move to a western country they look down upon the western culture! Why the fuck did they move there in the first place?!

What really pisses me off is the complete fear that our politicians and media show towards these animals! If these wankers don't like freedom of speech then tell the cunts to fuck off out of our country! Every time these people overreact to little things or fly planes into skyscrapers the first thing you will see on the telly is white people talking about the '*lovely Muslim moderates*' and how peaceful Islam is. The trouble is, you never actually see these so called moderate Muslims on TV because the fact is the majority of them sympathise with the terrorists themselves!

In schools a whole class or even year group can be punished because of the actions of one bad egg. It's a really successful method that teachers use to root out trouble makers. It's a system that works in lots of aspects of life. The Islam problem is easily solved, firstly stop allowing anymore Muslims to immigrate to our lands. Make mosques illegal buildings, ban the burka, persecute this religion so much that they have no option but to either denounce their faith or move back to a Muslim country.

People will say that Muslims are entrepreneurs and that a country can't have enough entrepreneurs. Trouble with Muslim's is they are greedy and the majority of them only deal in cash in hand businesses. Tax dodging cunts! As well as looking down on our society they don't contribute anything to it either! All they do is rape our wallets and underage white girls!

People will say that to insult Islam is like playing a game of Russian roulette…it could kill you. I'm not going to insult Islam, that would just be offensive. Instead I'm just going to tell the truth and anyone who is offended by truth…well, I wouldn't piss on that type of person even they were on fire! So here's the truth in one simple line,

ALLAH DOESN'T EXIST AND MOHAMMED WAS A FUCKING PAEDOPHILE!!

29
I HATE EVERYTHING!
PART THREE:
THE LAST RANT!

ENGLISH TOURISTS- Those of you who have read my first book will already know that I have a distaste for your typical English tourist but before I go any further I have a confession to make. When I was younger, I was your typical English tourist, probably worse than your typical English tourist actually. At the tender age of nineteen I went to Magaluf with eleven of my mates. We stayed in a hotel called the Fiesta Jungla, it was probably the roughest hotel on the island. On my very first morning after waking up I was approached by the hotel manager and immediately put on my final warning. *'Any behaviour like the night before and I would have to leave the hotel!'* Two separate club reps told me I was the most obnoxious man that they had ever met. If you think this is some sort of boast I can assure you it isn't, the thought of my behaviour on that holiday makes me cringe. I was a young boy full of vodka, that's my excuse anyway.

As we grow up we become wiser and quieter. The problem seems to be that not everyone does. If you're abroad and there's a loud drunken tit near you, you have a 90% chance of him being English. We are the world's most hated tourist and we don't even realise it. At home no one likes a loud cunt but this fact seems to be forgotten when we go abroad. These drunken English wankers think that by being loud and smarmy everyone will like them, are they fucking mad? Everyone just thinks they're a bellend!

In my last book I wrote how the Thai's don't really like us and I know that those comments will have infuriated some men who would argue blue in the face with me. It's the truth though, how can anyone expect a quiet race of people to like a loud race of people? That's why everyone hates the Yanks.

The problem we English have is our history, because at one time we ruled the world and now half the planet can speak our language we think that makes us superior somehow. That and a mix of the sea air. We think that people who live in coastal towns are a bit backwards but we forget that we are an island race. That makes us a bit different from our mainland cousins. So we go abroad, get drunk, we have our pride in our history and our backwards island mentality. What a lethal mixture! I know it's not all of us, I myself, think I'm a very good tourist these days but there is a lot of us who seem to be absolute wankers. They strut down the street in their England tops, with their British Bulldog tattoos on their legs and talking loudly so everyone can hear that they're

English. Who do these people think are going to be impressed?

There's a particular type of English tourist who seem to be even worse than the rest, those fucking Cockneys. Now the worst thing about Cockneys is, this isn't just a holiday mentality, it's their normal mentality. In England itself they think that anyone north of Watford isn't really English, they have a backwards patriotism which leads them to believe that they're the best race of people in the world. Cockneys do you really believe that you're the best? OK chaps, by the way you can keep your fucking ridiculous mortgages on your shoebox houses and tiny gardens. You fucking thick cunts!

We are lucky to be born in England but we aren't any better than anyone else.

SPICEBOYS/JACK THE LADS- Firstly if you don't know what a spiceboy is, it's a man who spends more time in front of a mirror than a woman. These are two different types of men but I've lumped them together because they share one huge thing in common. Their whole life is based on what everyone else thinks of them. They desperately want to be liked by everyone and this vanity obsession means they are just completely fake people.

Jack the lads are just tits. They will stand at a bar and talk as loud as they can so everyone in the room can hear them. Their fake swagger, their constant looking around to see who's listening to them! I can't get my head around anyone who wants strangers to listen into their private conversation. It's the height of attention seeking! (Or maybe that's writing a book about yourself)

Spiceboys make me feel sick, they are not real men. None of us like to leave our house looking scruffy but there is a limit to self-image. These idiots completely cross the line. I just can't take them seriously, they mince around in their tight jeans wearing their fucking manbag's giving it '*look at me*'. I would rather turn my back to one of them than have a conversation with them.

FEMENISTS- A few years ago a huge smile was put on my face! Women's car insurance and retirement age both shot up. Those fucking feminists finally got what they deserved! Now don't get me wrong dear reader, I've got nothing against women's rights, but I fucking hate feminists! What a pack of cunts they are!

They have completely destroyed the women of England. If I was to say 'It's a woman's job to raise her kids' I would be shot down as sexist pig by a feminist. But what they forget is that since the dawn of man, women have always looked after the kids whilst the men have gone out to provide. In fact that's how it still is for 90% of the families on earth this very day. It's called nature and feminists go completely against nature. It's only been in the last couple of decades that everything has completely changed in western countries.

The feminists demanded that every woman should seek out a career before they have kids. Due to that notion greedy mortgage lenders took advantage and introduced 'dual income' mortgages, which caused our house prices to triple over night! We are all crippled in debt and we have these stupid lesbian wankers to blame! From that then spawned expensive childcare and pensioners golden years being ruined by having to parent again.

I really can't believe the attitudes of women today. They won't even breastfeed anymore! I remember when my ex-wife was pregnant with our first child, her sister asked her,

"Are you going to breastfeed then?"

"Of course I am."

"Urghh! What are you going to do that for?!"

I bit my tongue at the time but really I felt like spitting in her face! What has happened to our women dear reader? Why do they feel the need to compete with us? Have we really been that bad to them? I'd love to tell a feminist to go and spend twelve hours cleaning a sewer, or erecting some scaffolding. At the end of the day when she was completely broken I'd say,

"Right, same again tomorrow…in fact same again every week for the rest of your working life!"

The magic of seeing her face drop as the reality of it dawned on her. Feminists are the most ungrateful creatures on earth. I blame our high divorce rate on them, our high house prices on them, in fact every single bad thing in our society I blame on feminists…even the shit weather!

TEXT/COMPUTER SPEAK- These are two different things that I hate for two different reasons. Text speak is sheer laziness! When I text people I make a point of spelling every word correctly, using proper grammar. (Although admittedly I probably haven't done either of those things in this book!) These stupid acronyms people use, LOL being the most popular. Who actually says LOL? Dickheads that's who! A few years ago a friend of mine finished a text with the acronym LMAO! I text back,

"What the fuck does that mean?"

"Laughing My Ass Off!" Was the reply.

"Ass? Are you American now you stupid cunt?!"

I have a way with words dear reader. There is no reason at all for misspelling words unless you are thick. Text speak is an open admittance that the person sending it is a fucking spastic.

Computer speak is even worse and it really boils my piss! I'm not a social media sort of person but I have looked on forums before. I don't know the reason why people do this but when they type words they start talking in a way that they would never do in real life. Basically they decide to go 'all American.' They use cheesy American words that serve absolutely no purpose in life. Why do it? Why don't they just speak with the language they've been brought up with? They just come across as complete geeks!

NON-VOTERS- If there's one good thing about working in construction it's the ability of us male workers to speak openly and freely with one another without fear of receiving any labels. Since I started working in construction the number one topic of conversation has been immigration. Even during the reign of Tony Blair's evil New Labour government, where anyone who talked about immigration was instantly labelled a racist, us construction workers had no such problem. I'm a realist, England needs immigrants, the country would fall to pieces without them. You already know that I don't like multiculturalism but immigration and multiculturalism are two completely different topics. (Although no doubt a do-gooder wouldn't be able to see the difference). All I ask from an immigrant workforce is that they speak our language, dress like us, adhere to our work regulations and laws and keep their religion out of the country. No foreigner in England should be entitled to any benefits at all and they should all have health insurance. These aren't racist comments, they are just common sense!

I hope to live in Thailand one day. In my four holidays so far I have learned 20+ Thai words, if I were to live there I would try my best to learn the language proper. I would need medical insurance as well, I would never begrudge these things I would just be happy that I was able to live in that country. My atheist views would be kept to myself and I would avoid at all costs doing anything to insult the Thai people. It's that simple saying all over again, *'When in Rome do as the Romans'*

In England we are not allowed to say '*we're full*' but that's the cold hard truth and there's no point in anyone denying it. The drawbridge needs to be pulled up, we've got to a point where we need an immigrant workforce to support the immigrants who are already here! I have never met a work colleague with a different view from my own, in fact most of them have very right-wing views on the subject and think I'm too liberal! Everybody talks politics, even if they don't realise they're doing it.

Every once and a while you meet a person and it doesn't take long for you to realise that you want to stop talking to them. For me it's the idiots who spend ten minutes talking about how fucked the country is and then they finish their rant by proudly stating that they have never voted and never will. I have always given these people a piece of my mind, no matter how big they are. All three major parties are exactly the same so people choose not to vote, fair enough but never ever talk politics with anyone.

It's my belief that everyone should be forced to vote, purely because of what our ancestors had to go through to get us the vote. If you are reading this and you don't vote but you are angry about the state of your country then please reconsider. You never have to vote for one of the three main parties but you can vote with your fist and make a protest. The masses are only allowed to talk about immigration these days because of the rise of UKIP. Their popularity means that serving politicians and news reporters can't duck the issue anymore, they HAVE to talk about it. If every single person did a protest vote we would see a radical change in this country. You don't even have to go to a polling station anymore, surely everyone has got the five minutes it takes to tick a box and post a letter?

LAWS BROKEN IN THE NAME OF RELIGION- Before you get worried that I'm going to rant on about wars and terrorism then don't, I won't waste my breath on shite like that! This chapter is about our own English laws that are allowed to be bent and completely broken by foreign religions within our country.

If you were to ever to walk onto a construction site there are some pretty basic laws everyone has to adhere to. Work boots, safety glasses and hard hat. If I break any of these simple rules I can be prosecuted.

Now I don't really want to moan about Sikh's because along with Buddhists they are one of the more peaceful religions BUT Sikhs are not required to wear hard hats on work sites! Because of their turbans they would find it pretty difficult to fit one on their head. If I take my hat off I will instantly lose my job but I'm expected to work alongside men who don't have to wear them! How does that work?! Surely that's prejudice towards the non-religious workers? Allow me to speak some common sense, if you can't take your fucking turban off then you don't get the job!

Recently halal and kosher meats have appeared in our news programmes. An English owned abattoir has to stun an animal before it is killed, that is the LAW! If the abattoir stopped doing this the owner would be thrown in prison. But foreign religion run abattoirs do not have to stun the animals. These fully conscious poor creatures have their throats slit and are left to bleed to death! When animal rights campaigners brought this story to the nation's attention there was only one way our ultra-left wing, Jewish ran media could report the story. They invited rabbis and imams onto the news to defend their case. I watched a few of these interviews and they all said the same thing, the animals have a much more peaceful death than in our abattoirs! I wish the news producers could have split the TV screen in two, the interviewee's talking about these 'peaceful deaths' on one side and the other side showing footage of the actual deaths. Dear reader,

I've heard that the horrific footage is available on YouTube if you have the stomach for it. I wonder what deaths the imams and rabbis would choose for their own children? Throat slit awake? Or throat slit unconscious? What do you think dear reader?

I keep coming back to this but 'when in Rome do as the Romans'. If you can't adhere to the laws of another country then fuck off back to where you came from. And if I hear one more story about a fucking Muslim checkout worker refusing to handle a bottle of wine I'll lose the plot! Go and tell your uncle to stop selling it in his fucking corner shop then, you thick cunt!

COMPETING MOTHERS- This is where I'm going to sound really old but I don't care. When I was a lad... our birthday parties consisted of five or six mates coming round your house. If the weather was nice you'd have a little party in the garden, if not it would be in the front room. The posh kids would have a McDonald's party. Cut to today and the change is unbelievable! Function rooms hired, food spreads ordered in, hired entertainers and fucking hundreds of kids!

I had the misfortune of attending my nephew's 5th birthday party in 2014. It was possibly the worst two hours of my life! My brother and his wife hired a church for the afternoon and there must have been around thirty of the loud little bastards running around. Worse than the kids though was the very loud children's entertainer! This bloke had his speakers turned up to eleven and he never once shut up. In my opinion a man must have something very wrong with his brain to choose that job as a profession. I would rather sell bags of cement for a living! My brother told me he had paid £400! That works out at £200 an hour, something I had great delight in telling him. I also told him he should've made his wife pay for it and that I would rather have cut my own hands off if it had been me!

So why these big extravagant parties? I said in my last book that western women spend their whole lives pretending. When they are kids they pretend to be adults and then when they do become adults they pretend to be of a higher class than what they really are. It's this ambition in life to be perceived as 'middle class' that has made these parties become the monsters that they are today. *"If 'Mrs. Jones' does that for her kid then I'll have to go one better!"* Trouble is where will it end? Will we have out of work z-grade celebrities parachuting through the ceilings next? Will the kids be forced to jump through rings of fire to win an electric car?

Its sheer fucking madness and we only have the competing mothers to blame…that and the completely spineless husbands who say 'yes dear.'

'BRITISH' PEOPLE- In this book I have tried to use the words British and Britain as sparingly as possible. I have used them only when I have felt the need to talk about us island brothers as a whole. I must admit dear reader, that I do not like the term 'British.' I am an Englishman and it seems in this modern society people don't like calling themselves English anymore.

The vast majority of people in England will only ever have one or two jobs in their life. They will not mix with as many people as what some of us do. They will have their Monday to Friday jobs 52 weeks of the year and they will listen to what the government and do-gooders tell them to, just like the good little citizens that they are. If only the majority of English people would broaden their horizons they would realise that in Wales and Scotland they are hated.

The hate isn't real of course, it's one of those border rivalries that every person in every region, council and country has. If the three of us were mixed together in a restaurant the majority of us all would get along. But the fact remains that it's only the English who call themselves British. A sweaty sock calls himself a Scotsman and a sheep rapist call himself a Welshman. To many English people nowadays if you say the words *'I'm English'* they will look at you as if you have just swore at them or even spat on them! What has happened to us?

On my very first trip offshore I worked alongside an Englishmen who came out with two lines that I will never forget.

"By the time I get home my lasses fanny will be biting the top of her leg off!"

And

"I'm not English! I'm British!"

It's the last line that sticks with me most. Although the first line was very funny there's no way that that ignorant, thick cunt could've come up with it himself. In those five short words he summed up everything that is wrong with modern day England. Now believe me dear reader, I don't class myself as a patriot and I believe that patriotism causes a lot of problems in the world BUT when a man gets to a point when he is afraid to declare his own nationality in his own country then something really, really horrible must have happened. I can't think of any other nation on earth with the same predicament.

I'm not an expert on these things but I'm fairly confident that not too long ago English people called themselves English. I was a child during the Maggie Thatcher years so I can't remember how we classed ourselves then but I became a man in the Tony Blair years and I know exactly how it was then. We were stripped of our identity and we were stripped of our culture. The people of Wales and Scotland don't even know about our dilemma, to them we are just '*the fucking English!*' They don't realise that the vast majority of English people do not share the same border rivalries as they do and that the vast majority of English people don't even class themselves as English, they class themselves as British. Could it be that the Welsh and Scots would actually feel sorry for us if they knew this fact? Absolutely not! They would just laugh and call us '*thick English cunts!*'

My fellow countryman, we are not thick and in our history we have never been cowards, let's never abandon our culture and let's never abandon our name!

30
WHO IS BARRY J STEEL?

Dear reader, I've had a strange fascination with the name Barry for a number of years now. I can remember after the birth of my son I said to my wife at the time,

"Who in their right mind could look at a beautiful new born baby and say, let's call him Barry?"

Now if you're called Barry trust me I'm not having a dig at you, it's not your fault. When I came up with my pseudonym it was the first name that popped into my head. There's one big problem about using a pseudonym and that's that you don't get to tell anyone that you've actually written a fucking book! The feeling of getting my first paperback delivered through my letter box was a magical little moment in my life and only ten people got to know about it! My family and most of my friends don't about Barry. For obvious reasons I don't want my family to know and as far as my mates are concerned, they're just typical men, their lips are far too loose.

The people who know me, know that I have absolutely no shame whatsoever! The reason I have my pen name is because I NEVER EVER want my kids to read my books. If anyone were to read this book and think they know my real identity then I ask you to please keep it to yourself.

If there's ONE MORE thing I hate in life dear reader, its fame hungry idiots. I am the type of man who spots someone I know in a supermarket and immediately heads for the opposite isle. I hate small talk with people I know and it would be my worst nightmare to have to have small talk with somebody that I didn't know!

I see writing as a hobby and I know my hobby will never bring me money, I'm destined to wear a boiler suit for the rest of my life. But I am a human being though and sometimes it's hard not to fantasise about what it would be like to be a full time author. One thing I would never wish for though is fame and I really can't understand the people in the world who crave it. Why would a person want to give up their privacy? Surely it's bad enough just having to say hello to your neighbours, never mind walking out of your house to a mob of unemployed weirdo's every day!

What I'm trying to say dear reader, is I would absolutely love my books to sell by the bucket load and turn writing from a hobby into a job but I will never want people to know who I am. If you have read this book and enjoyed it, please just enjoy the mystery and don't start a mission to find out who I am. I don't know how I come across in my books but if you imagine me to be some jolly, sociable, happy go lucky type who loves to court a crowd, then you need to know that I'm the complete opposite. If you were to ever meet me in real life I'm pretty sure that you would only find me to be a disappointment!

I know what some of you may be thinking right now…*'That front cover is a fucking con!'* In all honesty you'd be right! I want you to go back to the contents page and read through those chapter titles again and tell me what I was supposed to call this book? 'Load Of Shite!' wasn't an option by the way.

When I come up with my book titles I always google them first to make sure that they haven't been used before. As I was putting the finishing touches onto this book I decided to google some of my chapter titles. I was dismayed to find out that my two favourites had already been used in the past! 'The Origin of Faeces' and very fucking bizarrely 'Islam Ramadana Ding Dong'. I can assure you now that I had no prior knowledge of either of these and I was absolutely gutted when I found out. Whenever I have borrowed anything I've made a point of telling you straight away.

I want to take this opportunity to apologise for the, more than a, handful of errors in my first book. (If you've spotted any in this, then put it down to me being sick of reading the fucking thing!) I had been in such excitement to get it published that I completely rushed the proof reading stage! I could amend all those mistakes but the mingebag in me doesn't want to pay the fees involved! They shall remain intact as a constant reminder to me that I'm not really an author…I'm a hairy arsed tradesman just like you!

I've got ideas for two more books at the moment. One of them is going to take me a couple years to write and the other one will cost me a small fortune to write. That latter book is wholly dependent on the sale of this book. Dear reader, my words are in your hands…

The End

ALL PROCEEDS FROM THIS BOOK
ARE DONTATED TO THE
B.J.STEEL PENIS ENLARGEMENT FUND

Marketing for the Slightly Uncertain